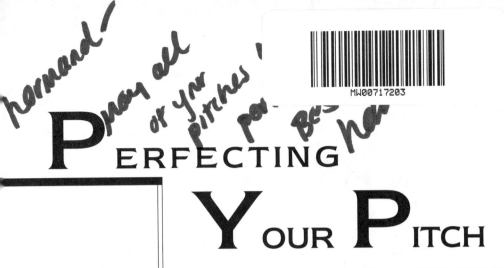

PERFECTING

YOUR PITCH

10 Proven Strategies for Winning the Clients Everyone Wants

By

Nancy Michaels

CAREER
PRESS

PERFECTING YOUR PITCH
EDITED BY CLAYTON W. LEADBETTER
TYPESET BY EILEEN DOW MUNSON
Front cover photo by Lynn McCann
Cover design by LogoWorks
Printed in the U.S.A. by Book-mart Press

Grow Your Business Network is a trademark of Impression Impact, Inc.

To order this title, please call toll-free 1-800-CAREER-1 (NJ and Canada: 201-848-0310) to order using VISA or MasterCard, or for further information on books from Career Press.

The Career Press, Inc., 3 Tice Road, PO Box 687,
Franklin Lakes, NJ 07417
www.careerpress.com

Library of Congress Cataloging-in-Publication Data

Michaels, Nancy, 1964-
    Perfecting your pitch : 10 proven strategies for winning the clients everyone wants / by Nancy Michaels ; foreword by Bruce Nelson.
        p. cm.
    Includes index.
    ISBN 1-56414-777-0 (paper)
    1. Marketing—Handbooks, manuals, etc. 2. Strategic planning—Handbooks, manuals, etc. 3. Success in business—Handbooks, manuals, etc. I. Title.

HF5415.M525 2005
658.8--dc22

                                                        2004057058

To Chloe, Noah, and Sophia—

My three little angels

who continue to "pitch" their ideas

better than anyone I know.

Acknowledgments

I am so blessed to have so many wonderful associates, colleagues, and friends in my life who helped bring this project to life. Rarely is something created from the efforts of one person—and in this case, there's no exception.

My parents, Tom and Catherine Staiti, have taught me the importance of honesty, integrity, and treating all people with respect and dignity. Not only have these lessons benefited me in my personal life, but in my professional career, as well. I'll always be grateful for their support, encouragement, and faith in me: My endless thanks and love to both of you.

Lindsey Pollak, my book coach and confidante on this project, is a must-have for anyone interested in writing a book. Her probing questions made me delve deeper into this topic and offer the reader breadth and depth on a subject near and dear to my heart. I consider Lindsay my friend, collaborator, and sounding board on all things book-related, and I am eternally grateful to her for bringing this project to fruition.

Brittany Albright, my ace assistant, exemplifies grace under pressure, extreme professionalism, and dedication to her work at Impression Impact. Brittany always makes me look my best and warrants the kind comments of all who connect with her at my office: I am indebted to you and so glad you're on my team.

Jennifer Flynn, my friend and colleague, is a sales pro who works by my side in our efforts to "pitch" new business and close more deals: I am so grateful to have you pleasantly persist with all incoming and pursued leads, and I'm grateful to have you as a travel companion on many of our sales trips. Thanks for going above and beyond the call of duty by offering your assistance on bad hair days, as well.

Sharron Kahn, my editor, graciously offers her assistance on a moment's notice and turns around a superior product every time: Thanks so much for your continued help and willingness to go the extra mile.

My sincere thanks go out to my clients at Office Depot. Bruce Nelson, who graciously agreed to write the Foreword to this book, has always been an advocate of my work and continues to support me and spread the word about our Grow Your Business Network. Monica Luechtefeld, with whom we work on Office Depot's Web Café, is not only one of the smartest women I know, but a wonderful mentor to me. It's a rare and wonderful find to have a client who you learn so much from: Thank you, Monica. Thanks also to Lynn Connelly and Valika Shircharran, for their support of my work and their commitment to better serve women business owners: It's been a joy and pleasure to work with you and your team.

My other corporate sponsors include Jeanne Wilson-Yu, Valerie Mason Cunningham, Rosie Madison, Diane McGarry, and Carol Dalesandro at Xerox; Janis Jarosz and Lisa Berardo at Cendant; Morgan Lynch and Adam Franks at LogoWorks, with a special thank you for designing this book cover and the Website (*www.perfectingyourpitch.com*); Gail Goodman, Steve Oriola, Janet Muto, and Eric Groves at Constant Contact; Harvey Bulter at JPMorgan Chase; Kathy Homeyer at UPS; and Sharon Hoffman-Avent of Smead, who support opportunities for me to speak to women and minority business owners—my favorite audience: I'm so grateful to you all.

My dear friend and colleague Jane Pollak has connected me to so many wonderful and helpful people. Not only did Jane introduce me to Lindsey, but she also made the most wonderful connection to her sister Meredith Bernstein—my extraordinary agent, whose intrigue, commitment, and initiative on this project has been unwavering: Many thanks, Meredith, for a superior job and getting this book out to the marketplace. I'm eternally grateful for your support.

Thanks to the team at Career Press—Mike Lewis; Kirsten Beucler; Stacey Farkas; Eric Goldwyn; and Ron Fry, President: You've been delightful to work with and always open to my endless list of ideas and selling strategies. I'm extremely grateful. A special thanks goes out to Clayton Leadbetter, my editor at CP, whose conscientious manner has made this book more accurate and readable: My sincere gratitude to you.

I would also like to thank my public relations team at Newman Communications—Dan Ratner and Tess Woods—for their expertise and dedication to promoting my book. A special thank you to my own publicist, Ginny Shea of Mixed Media, for her tireless efforts and willingness to "pitch" this book in new and unusual ways.

Susan Bari, at Women's Business Enterprise National Council, hired me to deliver Perfecting Your Pitch seminars to women-certified business owners. Susan and her staff, including Betty Cole, Linda Denny, and others at WBENC, planted the seed and supplied the inspiration behind this initiative: Many thanks to you all.

My friends are always a source of wisdom, comfort, and encouragement to me. Thanks to Sandra Williams for being my oldest friend who gets to hear all about my latest pitches—whether she wants to or not. To Mary Lou Andre, a kindred spirit and attentive listener to the good, the bad, and the ugly in my life: Thank you for being my sounding board and trusted friend. As well, I would like to thank my women business owner comrades who attended the Tuck Executive Program with me and who feed my soul and mind with their like-mindedness and the support they freely give.

Thanks to Nell Merlino, the creator of Take Our Daughters to Work Day and Count-Me-In, for her straightforward and honest advice and huge heart: I've loved working with you and your loan recipients through my coaching program. To my personal PR team of supporters I couldn't live without, including Lauren Garvey, Kathleen Kelly Stockham, Glynne Kalil, Rieva Lesonsky, and Carrie Fitzmaurice, who are supporters and promoters of my work: Thank you a thousand times over.

To Joan Pars, who helped me create a home and work environment that allows the creative juices to flow wherever I am: I'm so grateful for your good taste, mentorship, and love—the same to your wonderful husband, Harry, too.

I'm also very grateful to Rose and Jim Hart, for their never-ending love for my children and our family and for making it easy for me to pursue this project knowing how well cared for and loved my children are in their care. To Carina Korner, our German au pair, whose creative genius provides more activity and fun than should be allowed in one household: Many thanks for your love and commitment to our family—we're grateful.

To all of the women and minority business owners I've addressed at speaking engagements, coached, and worked with in the past: I gain inspiration, strength, and knowledge from you and the challenges of running a small business; thank you for sharing your experiences and growth opportunities with me.

The entrepreneurs who are featured in this book also deserve my thanks. It is only through examples and stories that the reader can learn concepts and apply them to their own business in ways that will bring success. A special thanks to Edie Fraser at Best Practices in Corporate Communications for her assistance in providing invaluable resources for this book. In addition, I'd like to thank so many endorsers of my work in the small business community, including Service Corps of Retired Executives (SCORE), Small Business Administration (SBA), Small Business Development Center (SBDC), International Franchise Association (IFA), Women's Leadership Exchange (WLE), Women Presidents' Organization (WPO), National Association of Female Executives (NAFE), National Association of Female Executives (NAFE), National Association of Women Business Owners (NAWBO), and American Business Women's Association (ABWA), where I have the audience I love to address and the vehicle to do so. I feel blessed to do the work I love to do, and these organizations make it so.

Contents

Foreword by Bruce Nelson 11

Introduction 13
    The Lunch of a Lifetime

Section I
Before the Pitch
21

Chapter 1 23
    Develop Your Unique Selling Proposition to
    Identify and Attract Your Top Prospects

Chapter 2 43
    Build Your Reputation and Relationships

Chapter 3 85
    The Approach: How to Connect With
    Decision-Makers

Chapter 4 109
    The Only Pre-Meeting Checklist You'll Ever
    Need

Section II
During: What to Do With Your 15 Minutes of Fame
119

Chapter 5 121
Pitch Your Prospect's Socks Off

Chapter 6 135
Submit an Outstanding Proposal

Section III
After: Creating Lifelong Customers
147

Chapter 7 149
Don't Peak Too Early: The Art of Gentle
Persistence

Chapter 8 161
The Art of Overdelivery

Chapter 9 179
Take the Testimonial One Giant Step Farther:
Create an Endorsement Campaign

Chapter 10 197
Lifelong Marketing

Afterword 225

Appendix: Perfecting Your Pitch Top-10 Lists 227

Index 245

About the Author 251

Foreword

Business owners and independent professionals comprise a large segment of the U.S. population for several reasons. Independent-minded visionaries who embrace the challenge of running a business have represented the majority of entrepreneurs for centuries. These entrepreneurs have since been joined by individuals seeking career alternatives in response to layoffs, downsizing, or inflexible work cultures. In addition, technological advances have made it easier for the small business to compete with—and sell to—large corporations. The dream of owning a business has become a reality for millions of Americans.

Individuals turn to entrepreneurship as a way to control their own destiny, balance their work and family lives, and fulfill their dreams. At Office Depot, I have witnessed the relentless spirit of entrepreneurs as they seek to distinguish themselves by becoming experts in their fields and surpassing every customer expectation. Nancy Michaels, the author of this book, distinguished herself with me by bidding $1,050 at a charity auction to lunch with me and share her great idea for in-store customer seminars for Office Depot.

Succeeding in business today presents a formidable challenge. As entrepreneurs, you're required to wear many hats. You often serve as accountant, lawyer, business strategist, marketer, technology expert, administrator, human resource manager, and of course, salesperson. The ability to pitch your business successfully while playing so many roles is difficult but critical.

Perfecting Your Pitch offers inspiring stories and real-life examples of ways that you can "perfect your pitch" and grow your business. The visionaries featured in this book are shining examples of individuals who did their homework, saw past immediate obstacles, remained committed to their dreams, and found ways to stand out above the competition. Creativity and drive, not money, is the key to success in every story and example.

Reading this book will inspire, motivate, and guide you to achieve more than you've ever dreamed possible for your business. But don't just read *Perfecting Your Pitch*—use the ideas it presents to yield immediate and long-term results.

—Bruce Nelson
Chairman and CEO,
Office Depot, Inc.

The Lunch of a Lifetime

It happened like this: A friend and colleague introduced me to her daughter, who introduced me to a former coworker, who introduced me to a prospect and recommended an event I should attend, where I met a board member and influencer of my dream *Fortune* 500 client prospect, where I heard a speaker mention a silent auction, where I bid on lunch with the then CEO of the company I was targeting, which I won, that led to lunch, where I pitched my dream project to my dream CEO prospect, who loved the idea and invited me to give a formal pitch to his team, which I did, that led to the biggest contract of my business career.

Phew! I'm exhausted just thinking about it.

What on Earth am I talking about? This is the story of how I won Office Depot—my dream prospect—as a client and what I learned from the process. I believe that any motivated, credible, passionate business owner or independent professional can use similar tactics to win new business from dream clients. How? By perfecting the preparation, presentation, and follow-up of your *pitch*.

Let me share with you the story of how I pitched and won Office Depot as a client. I believe in the "six degrees of separation" theory and often tell my clients or participants in my seminars that we all have access to whomever we choose to pursue. If you went through your

Rolodex and called the 10 contacts you thought might have the best chance of reaching your desired prospect, chances are, they would know someone who knows someone who is best friends with that specific person. This is how I was able to reach Bruce Nelson, CEO of Office Depot.

A dear friend of mine, Jane Pollak, was on my speaker team when we were conducting several in-store seminars, for a leading retailer, on ways for small business owners to effectively market themselves. I love Jane and she's never led me down a dead-end path. She's a gifted artist, author, and speaker, and I trust her implicitly. She introduced me to her daughter, Lindsey, who, at the time, worked for a women's business Website. We clicked, and I saw Lindsey at a weekend retreat at Canyon Ranch, where Jane, Lindsey, and I escaped for some R and R. Lindsey told me that her friend and former coworker, Betsy Myers, was moving to my hometown of Boston and I should connect with her.

I met Betsy for breakfast in Cambridge, where she was then the Alumni Director at the Kennedy School of Government at Harvard. Like Jane and Lindsey, I clicked with Betsy. Betsy then told me about a woman at Office Depot named Lynn Connelly, who organizes their conference for women business owners and said I had to attend if I was interested in landing Office Depot as a client.

With Betsy's blessing, I contacted Lynn Connelly, signed up for the conference, and attended in January 2002. Lo and behold, at the conference, I met Nancy Evans, cofounder of iVillage, in the elevator on the way to the opening speaker's presentation. I started a conversation with her and eventually showed Nancy my pitch materials (that I had brought with me) and explained the work I had done for another retailer. She seemed impressed and offered to make personal introductions to Lynn Connelly and Office Depot's CEO and Chairman, Bruce Nelson. It turned out that Nancy is on Office Depot's Women's Advisory Board. Serendipity!

While waiting for the conference's opening speaker to begin, a woman walked onstage to announce a silent auction in which the highest bidder would win lunch with Bruce Nelson. I filed the information in the back of my head and then, one minute before the auction closed that afternoon, I outbid the last bid by $50 and plunked down my AmEx Platinum card for a $1,050 lunch with Bruce Nelson. My colleagues thought I was crazy to bid so high, but I knew that if I had Mr. Nelson's ear over lunch, I could easily sell him on the idea of doing in-store consumer seminars for Office Depot's small business customers. Luckily (except for my AmEx bill!), I won the lunch, Bruce went for the idea, and several meetings and conversations later, we had a solid project to roll out in six months.

The timeline looked like this from when I attended the conference to the moment I secured the business...

My CEO Lunch Timeline

1/20/02 Attend the Success Strategies for Women Conference sponsored by Office Depot in Boca Raton, Florida.

1/22/02 Bid on lunch with Bruce Nelson, Office Depot's CEO, during a silent auction—and win!

2/6/02 Bruce Nelson calls my cell phone to schedule lunch for March 8, 2002.

3/8/02 Bruce and I have lunch at Sundy Beach Restaurant in Delray Beach, Florida, from 11:30 am–1:30 pm. I pitch in-store seminar idea.

3/17/02 Send Bruce a written proposal to conduct a pilot program to do in-store consumer seminars for Office Depot's small business customers on the topic of creative marketing strategies.

5/07/02 Bruce refers me to Jerry Colley, Office Depot's President of North American Stores, and Jerry calls me to arrange an appointment in Boston at Logan Airport the following Friday.

5/16/02   Meet with Jerry, Jim Petit, Tru Hall, and other members of the Office Depot team at Logan Airport to pitch them on the idea presented to Bruce.

5/29/02   Fly to Delray Beach, Florida, Office Depot's headquarters, to meet with Mike Burkette and Venna Tredway to discuss this pilot program. Test dates are slated for September.

6/2/02   Send a press release out to the media outlining my CEO lunch experience as a creative marketing strategy to win an account. The phone rings from *USA Today*, *Oprah*, and *The Boston Globe*.

6/6/02   Speak with George Naddaff, founder of Boston Chicken (now Boston Market)—mentor and friend—who thinks the CEO Lunch idea could be a winning business model. My adrenaline gets revved up and I start to make some calls.

6/13/02   After meeting with George Naddaff, Peter Senne, and Emilie Marks at their offices, George agrees to be on my advisory board and donate a lunch for me to auction off for charity. Peter and Emilie want to help as well.

          Call Bruce Nelson, to enlist his support and fill him in on the potential PR opportunities. He agrees to be on the board of this new company—and donate a lunch, too.

Here is the press release I sent to the media to announce the success of my pitch:

FOR IMMEDIATE RELEASE

MAY I BUY YOU A $1,000 LUNCH...MR. CEO?

Silent Auction Bid Nets Small Business Expert Nancy Michaels Lunch With Office Depot Chairman and CEO and Eventual Seminar Series

MAY 2002, BOCA RATON, FLA.—Creative marketing techniques have long been a key component in entrepreneur Nancy Michaels' bag of strategy. From celebrating non-traditional holidays like Chinese New Year to steadfastly denouncing the usefulness of a company brochure, she continually looks for a different approach that will help her reach her clients more effectively. But recently even Michaels surprised herself a little by bidding over $1,000 at The Success Strategy for Business Women Conference sponsored by Office Depot—just to have lunch with Office Depot Chairman and CEO Bruce Nelson.

"It was important for me to meet Mr. Nelson," said Michaels, founder of Impression Impact of Concord, Massachusetts. "I wanted to assess his interest in small business seminars.... Was it a risk? Absolutely."

According to Michaels, her colleagues sitting with her at her table thought she was crazy to bid so high, but Michaels had to find a creative way to pitch her idea for the giant office supplier to host in-store marketing seminars for small businesses. The high-priced lunch with Bruce Nelson led to Michaels contacting Jerry Colley, Office Depot's President of North American Stores, and persistently following up until a meeting was scheduled. After several meetings, Nelson and Colley recognized the benefits of the idea, and Michaels is set to deliver her first series starting this fall in Boca Raton, Florida.

Designed to assist small businesses in their marketing efforts, the *What You Need to Know* Small Business Seminars are 90 minutes long and will be hosted in conference rooms at various Office Depots. Michaels, a well-known national speaker and entrepreneur, will present six creative elements for marketing—Develop your MSA (Major Selling Advantage); Create memorable marketing materials; Design a promotional kit *not* a costly brochure; Establish a cost-effective direct mail campaign; Develop a professional, effective web presence; and Become "Off The Wall" in your marketing efforts. The business marketing seminars will be presented for a nominal fee to entrepreneurs, small business owners, and interested members of the public.

"Nancy's knowledge of the small business market and her creative approach will benefit both customers and our stores," said Nelson, chairman and CEO of Office Depot. "The *What You Need to Know* Small Business Seminars will provide valuable information to a large segment of our customer base."

Michaels was quick to note that although the initial lunch with Nelson was the most expensive lunch she ever had, all the money went to a charity—Count Me In—which champions the cause for women's economic independence by providing access to business loans, consultation, and education. Her creative spirit is ready to help Office Depot's customers develop their own creative marketing strategies.

"I don't think I'll recommend a lot of expensive client lunches," said Michaels, "but I recognized the opportunity and the creative and risk-taking aspects of the experience will certainly be something I advocate to small business owners."

Based in Concord, Massachusetts, Impression Impact provides creative marketing strategies for businesses, large and small, to help them reach their optimal sales. You can visit Michaels by going to www.impressionimpact.com.

What is the lesson from this story? Had I simply picked up the phone and tried to get through to Bruce Nelson to pitch him my in-store seminar idea, it may or may not have worked. And at any step of the long process, from meeting Jane Pollak to beginning my contract with Office Depot, I could have faltered, lost confidence, and missed out on the best sale of my career.

Now that I've sketched the outline of my "perfect pitch," the rest of this book will fill in the details and help you perfect *your* pitch. I will tell you:

- How I determined that Office Depot was my dream client.

- What I said when I called Betsy Myers, Lynn Connelly, and others for the first time.

- What I said to Nancy Evans in the elevator (my "elevator pitch") at the Office Depot conference.

- What pitch materials I had with me at the conference (and have with me all the time).

- Everything you always wanted to know about lunching with the CEO of one of America's biggest companies: what I wore, what we chose for chitchat, what I ordered, what fork I used, what materials I brought to the meeting, and how I pitched my idea. Believe me, it all matters!

- How I followed up with Bruce Nelson (and how I got through his assistant).

- How I presented my formal pitch to the team at Office Depot.

- How I closed the deal.

- How I used this story to win publicity and additional clients.

Perfecting Your Pitch will appeal to any business professional look-ing to develop new clients or customers. This broad audience includes salespeople in all fields, real estate brokers, insurance agents, financial planners, professional speakers, small business owners, consultants, and many other professionals.

At the end of this book, I have included an appendix of top-10 lists (my signature pieces). These lists contain 10 critical points from each chapter. I encourage you to keep them handy and review them before, during, and after your pitch process. The top-10 lists are useful if you need to solve a specific problem or if you need a quick reminder of the most important points.

As you can see, perfecting your pitch is far more complex than just writing a proposal and popping it in the mail to a prospective client. There are hundreds of important steps that all add up to a perfectly executed, successful business pitch. You need to recognize opportuni-ties, be open to them, and pursue them with energy, intelligence, and vision.

Throughout the book you will read stories of many "overnight suc-cesses" that took nothing short of several months or several years to achieve!

And, as you know, the rewards can be enormous.

Now, are you getting hungry for lunch?

Section

I

Before the Pitch

Chapter 1

Develop Your Unique Selling Proposition to Identify and Attract Your Top Prospects

If you are a business owner or salesperson, you are always on the verge of a pitch, whether you know it or not. Maybe you've lost your biggest client and need to find new business. Perhaps you're maxed out with orders when the phone rings, and it's the largest player in your field calling to ask you to branch out in an entirely new (and highly lucrative) direction. These things happen. The question is, how do you take advantage of them? This book will show you how. In the pages to follow, you will learn to recognize that moment you've been waiting for, move quickly, and make the perfect pitch.

In the world of perfect pitches, my most recent "Danger, Will Robinson!" moment occurred while working on a five-year strategy with a business planning consultant. There I was, with all of my folders spread before me, when I suddenly realized that I had only one client! Granted, it was a huge, *Fortune* 500 client with several subsidiaries and franchisees, but still, it was one client! My entire livelihood was in the hands of a single company. You know that saying about putting all your eggs in one basket? Well, I had one egg in one basket. I knew this was a dangerous position, and I knew I had to do something about it. I had to change my approach and diversify my client base. I had to identify new clients and perfect not just one pitch, but many.

What do I do during a crisis like this? I lift my eyes to the wall above my desk, where a small framed print of the Chinese symbol for "crisis" hangs. It's made up of Chinese characters that, separately, represent "danger" (no surprise there) and "opportunity." Whenever I look at that print, I'm reminded that the challenge in any crisis is to find the opportunity and remember that there is *always* opportunity. In this case, it helped me to remember that there are always new clients to pitch. This symbol is a reminder to me that marketing is about training your brain to see opportunities where others may not see them. What opportunity is visible to me that nobody else is seeing, that I can take advantage of?

Few (meaning *no*) small business owners I know have their own personal scout, searching out new opportunities for them. They have to do it themselves. In other words, they hardly do it at all. Frankly, small business owners are busy people who work themselves silly just keeping their companies profitable. The only time many of them search out new business is when they find themselves facing a crisis. There's no need to wait. If you train yourself to identify new opportunities—even when you don't need the business—your payback will be to never again worry that your business is growing stale.

The USP

Early on in my business, I used to believe that everyone was a potential prospect. It's good to have confidence, but unless you're selling toothpaste (or a similarly wide-reaching consumer product), chances are, your ideal client list is a bit more limited—or targeted. Rather than trying to reach everyone and getting only a few, target your pitch by identifying the characteristics of your ideal client. Once you know who those companies or customers are, you can begin to develop relationships with them. You probably already know or do business with many of these companies. But you'll be surprised how many more prospects you can identify through a few simple exercises.

> The first step in perfecting your pitch is:
> **Identify your ideal client.**

There are several questions you should ask yourself to help identify your ideal client:

Who

- Who have I worked with in the past? This group includes clients, volunteer groups, board memberships, networking contacts, volunteers, board members, and speakers at industry events.
- Who is the customer base of my ideal client? Are those clients potential customers of mine as well?
- What size company would I most like to do business with?
- What type of people do I best interact with?

What

- What are my strengths?
- What are my areas of expertise?
- What are my most successful business achievements, and what type of clients have benefited the most?
- How will I save my clients money?
- What am I most passionate about?

When

- Am I ready for bigger clients? New directions?
- In what time frame do I want to work with new clients?

Where

- What is the ideal location for my clients? (For many people this is no longer relevant, but it is crucial for businesses such as repair services or one-on-one counseling.)

Why

- Why am I compelled to work in this area?
- What do I find myself studying and reading?
- Why am I different? Why should I be the dream vendor for my dream client? Know what makes you special and never forget it!

By answering these questions you are in the process of developing a *unique selling proposition* (USP) for your business. My friend and small business expert Mark LeBlanc refers to this as your "defining statement"; Nell Merlino, founder of Take Our Daughters to Work Day (whose story I will share later in this book), calls this your "major selling advantage." No matter what you call it, you need a statement that clearly demonstrates the unique product or service only *you* can bring to your client base. If you can clearly articulate your unique selling proposition, you will attract clients that want to buy what you sell.

Here is a simple formula for determining your unique selling proposition. Your goal with the USP is to clarify who you work with and explain what results you deliver. Be as bottom-line driven as you can.

Formula for creating a defining statement or major selling advantage to potential clients:

I work with _____ who want _____.

Try to keep your USP under 15 to 20 words. Here are some examples:

*I work with **large companies** who want **to increase their business with small companies.***

—Nancy Michaels, Impression Impact

*I work with **adults** who want **a pain-free experience when they go to the dentist.***

—Dentist

*I work with **non-fiction authors** who want **a guaranteed-to-sell book proposal.***

—Freelance Writer and Book Proposal Expert

*I work with **high-income ($500,000-plus) women** who want **to reach their retirement dreams as quickly as possible.***

—Independent Financial Planner

Repeat your USP over and over again. Frame it and hang it above your desk. Live it every day. You can revise it as necessary, but always know who you are, who your customers are, and what you can do to reach their needs. Of course this exercise has only introduced you to the *profile* of your ideal prospect. Now it's time to put a face (or two or 100) to the profile you've developed. It's time to research the "who."

A Step-By-Step Guide to Researching Prospects

In today's wired world, there is absolutely no excuse for not being a research genius. There is very little information you *can't* find on the Internet these days, yet I am still amazed when I learn that businesspeople enter a pitch meeting without fully researching a prospect company—and the personal and professional history of everyone at the meeting. It sounds a bit scary, but it's true: You cannot only find prospects, but also learn crucial facts about those prospects simply by typing their names into Google.com. In fact, I have a young friend who won't agree to a date until she "Googles" the prospect!

Here is a step-by-step plan for developing a list of real companies and people who fit the "who" described in your unique selling proposition.

Step 1: Develop a Comprehensive Database

You must have a comprehensive database to keep track of your new business prospects. These don't necessarily have to be current prospects, but may be companies you'd like to target several years down the road. You should be researching new prospects all the time, so be sure to collect all of this information in a central place where you can access it when you need it—when the crisis/opportunity arises. I recommend two storage "areas" for contact information: one on your computer for electronic copies, and one for hard copies.

Computer

I highly recommend the Best Software ACT! contact management database (visit *www.act.com* for purchasing information) for keeping track of your contacts. Others prefer to use Microsoft Outlook or to develop their own system. The important thing is to have a system that allows you to enter notes about each contact. You'll want to keep track not only of contact information, but also of phone conversations, articles, events attended together, and other "personal" connections with each contact.

Hard Copies

The good old-fashioned file cabinet is perfect. Develop a file for each contact/prospect and alphabetize away. If a contact's file gets too big, don't hesitate to start "Bill Gates II"—don't be stingy when it comes to information that might help in a later pitch.

■

I do not recommend buying a database of contacts that fit your ideal client profile. It's far better to develop your own proprietary list. While "bought lists" can be helpful in direct marketing campaigns, they are not the best way to find new clients. Remember, this is not a numbers game—it's a game of relationships and personal connections. In a highly personal business, such as financial planning, for instance, most new clients come through referrals, so a list of random strangers is virtually useless.

Here is the information you'll want to develop about your database of prospects…and where to find this information:

- **Date of any and all interactions.** Note the date you enter this person into your database (and why). Document any and all subsequent contact. This way you can refer to specific conversations or face-to-face interactions if necessary.

- **General contact information.** Include all phone numbers, fax numbers, the mailing address, and office location. Do not abuse this information (such as home phone numbers), but it's always a smart idea to have it.

  - This information can be found via the company's Website, an industry association database (see "Become Meaningfully Involved in Your Industry Association," on page 34), or by calling the company and asking the receptionist to provide as much information as possible.

  - When you do have an interaction with your contact, note how you got through—it's good information for the future!

- **Assistant's name and contact information.** With high-level contacts, you are most likely to interact with the person's assistant. The assistant may just become your best friend.

- **Articles written by or about each contact.** You can find these articles through general online searches (such as Google and Yahoo) and by setting up a keyword search on the contact's name at popular Websites such as *www.NewYorkTimes.com*. Some keyword searches charge a small fee; others are free. Of course you will also find articles when you read newspapers, magazines, and journals. Hard copies can go in your file cabinet.

- **Personal information**.
  - Family status.
  - Current residence(s).
  - Hometown.
  - Schools attended.
  - Past positions. Most industries are very incestuous. People also move around a lot, so you may have connections from a contact's former company.
  - Association memberships.
  - Volunteer activities.
  - Board memberships (for profit and nonprofit).
  - Hobbies.
  - Photograph.
  - Children's names and ages.

When Should You Buy a List?

The list that you create on your own is the best list, but if you are targeting a niche market, it may be worth buying a list. For instance, if you are marketing to franchisees, you may join the IFA (International Franchise Association) and use that list or buy a list of members. But you really have to be committed if you choose this path. Chances are, a more organic list will require less time to make the right impression, but a purchased list can work if you are committed to multiple points of contact. There is an advertising rule of thumb that it takes six impressions before your prospect can identify you.

Do be careful with purchasing e-mail lists, because SPAM rules are extremely strict.

Let's use my own company's USP and explore the information I gathered about a potential contact: *I work with large companies who want to increase their business with small companies.*

One company I identified as a "dream" prospect was a large financial services firm. Let's call it Financial Company X. A huge company, yes, but one that fit my criteria due to its recent emphasis on acquiring more small business customers for a new division. I learned about this new strategy through a press release on the company's Website.

I decided to start at the top, placing Financial Company X's CEO—we'll call him Mr. K—in my contact database. Mr. K is in the news frequently, so I quickly built up a file of articles on his business practices, but I wanted more personal information. I wanted to learn more about what Mr. K and I might have in common.

Here is what I learned from a simple Internet search:

◪ Mr. K is an African-American man, living in a small suburb north of New York City.

(Hmmm…my in-laws live in that same suburb.)

◪ He belongs to the Arts Council in that town.

(Perhaps I have some artist contacts involved with that organization?)

◪ Mr. K attended an alternative school for grades K–12.

(My daughter Chloe attends a branch of that same alternative school here in the Boston area.)

When I approach Mr. K in a letter or in person, these are some of the commonalities I will include. I can tell him that I feel a connection to him because of these similarities, and it is the truth. Relationships—the core of business—are built on connections.

What do you have in common with your prospects? Find out!

By the way, it is perfectly fine to have one of your employees perform the majority of this research, as long as you provide clear and detailed instructions. If you don't have employees, hire a college student to help. Sometimes younger people are gutsier in their research and cold-calling tactics, so take advantage of their lack of inhibition!

Step 2: Be a Secret Shopper

Surprisingly, many smart businesspeople who pitch their products or services to a large company overlook the most obvious form of research—the kind I like to call "research unplugged." It's the live, in-person, real-world research that you can't accomplish from the safety of your office chair. If your prospect is a retail store, shop there. If your prospect is a cosmetics line, wear it. If your prospect is a production company, see their films. If your prospect is a local bank, visit their ATMs and bank tellers. If your prospect makes pencils, use them whenever you write. At the very least, you should call and ask for the annual report of every company you are targeting (many annual reports are available online as well).

By using this key research strategy, you will learn more than you can ever imagine and you will avoid costly mistakes. Don't lose Xerox as a client because you bring your Hewlett-Packard laptop to the big pitch meeting! I have heard of this happening before.

When performing your real-world research, try to find answers to the following questions:

- What challenges does this company face?

- How does this company fare at customer service? Do you have ideas for improving it?

- Does the company appear to practice what it preaches, such as customer service, friendliness, and so on?

- Who are the competitors of this company? Perhaps there is another dry cleaner directly across the street from the one whose PR business you'd like to win. Perhaps both dry cleaners are potential clients, or perhaps you can try the services of both to see which proprietor needs your services more urgently.

- What is the company's stock price (if it's a public company), and how does that price compare to the previous year?

Take notes every time you visit a location, call the company, or have any other interaction. Don't forget to enter your findings in your database. This is information that senior-level executives will value when you are pitching your services for improving their current practices.

If your top prospects are individuals rather than companies, your real-world research should involve visiting the places your prospects visit and understanding their day-to-day experiences. Make notes about your experiences and how your product or service can improve the lives of your potential clients. You need to walk your talk—know what your clients know.

Step 3: Subscribe to Essential Publications

I know what you're thinking: All of this research is great, but information changes so quickly these days, how will I ever keep up? The answer is that you have to surround yourself with ongoing sources of information, aka reading material. How do you find out who you need to know and what those people know? Read what they read. Read what they write for. Read what they want to be quoted in. Read *everything*.

Here is a brief list of what you should be reading on a regular basis. I recommend setting aside about 30 minutes a day to skim all of your information sources. You don't have to read every article, but you do need to scan for relevant information about prospects, potential prospects, competitors, and trends. Be sure to add any relevant writers or editors to your contact database.

Essential Information Sources for Prospecting

☐ Trade publications—your industry and your prospects' industries.

☐ Major national newspaper.

☐ Community newspaper.

☐ Business magazines (*Fortune, Forbes, Fast Company, Inc.,* and so on, depending on your field).

☐ Your prospect's online newsletters and press releases (sign up for these in the "media" section of the company's Website).

☐ Your competitors' e-newsletters and press releases—create a new "anonymous" e-mail address for yourself, if necessary!

Step 4: Become Meaningfully Engaged in Professional Organizations

It is tempting and fabulously safe to sit in your office all day, re-searching every detail of every prospect, filling your numerous files, reading every trade journal and newspaper in sight, then sneaking out at lunchtime to stealthily roam the aisles of your prospects' retail out-lets for information that will help with your big pitch. But with this strat-egy, you're missing the most important component of prospecting: human connection.

Despite all of the amazing technology we now have at our fingertips, nothing will ever replace face-to-face relationship building. You can—and should—do as much research as you possibly can to know as much as you possibly can about your prospects, but in the end, the success of your pitch comes down to a combination of what you know about your pros-pects and *what your prospects know about you*. You must make yourself visible in your prospects' world. How do you make yourself visible? By showing up in the places where your top prospects are bound to be.

I have an easy formula for determining where you need to position yourself and your business to attract the attention of your prospects. Simply read back a few pages. Where did you look for information about your prospects? What publications did you read to learn the hot trends in your industry? What organizations do your prospects belong to? Voilà! These are the search engines, publications, and organizations where you need to be, too.

Professional associations are generally the best place to start. Every town and city has them, and while you may not be able to make the cover of *The Wall Street Journal* like Mr. K, you can certainly join orga-nizations of which he is a member. If your top prospects are individuals or smaller businesses, you're likely to meet them at industry functions and association events. If your top prospects are *Fortune* 500 CEOs such as Mr. K (who rarely attend association events themselves), you can rest assured that some of your prospect's top employees, custom-ers, vendors, and competitors will be in attendance—and these are all people you want to know as well.

While any association membership builds your network and increases your professional credibility, the best strategy is to join two different types of professional organizations:

1. Associations in your industry for peer support and best practices.

2. Associations in your prospects' industry (or industries) for education and new business prospecting.

I recommend that you join at least two or three associations, and be an active member. Don't join so many organizations that you don't have time to attend any of their events—this is why I use the word "meaningfully" engaged!

Recommendations for Becoming Meaningfully Involved in Professional Organizations in Your Industry

☐ Connect with the association leadership. Make yourself known to the people by planning events, editing the newsletter, and choosing speakers.

☐ If possible, access the full membership list of the association to find potential mentors and prospects. Most organizations publish a directory, which will be a key resource for your prospect files. If you can't get a full directory, learn names by reading the association's Website and publications, then use your standard research methods to learn more about the people featured.

☐ Attend events. You've heard the Woody Allen quotation before and I'll say it again: "Eighty percent of success is showing up." So get out there!

☐ Volunteer. Join a committee made up of the people you want to meet. There is no better way to prove your talent, commitment, and skills than to let people see you shine. Build up your resume with volunteer activities related to a recognized association.

☐ Offer to speak at events or contribute to association publications. This is the best way to be visible to other members, and to gain their respect.

☐ Send any press releases or "good news" items (such as a new client, new employee, or industry award) to your association. Many organizations publish "members on the move" types of columns that people love to read. Don't be shy.

☐ Find moral support. Never underestimate the importance of support. (See Chapter 2 for more suggestions on connecting with important people.)

Special Opportunities for Women and Minority Business Owners

If you are a woman or minority business owner, consider joining an organization that will help you secure certification of your business status. While certification is not a magic guarantee, it can give you a leg up against the competition when you are pitching major corporations or government agencies that seek certified businesses as suppliers for the supplier diversity initiatives. (For more information about certification and its benefits, contact the Women's Business Enterprise National Council [WBENC] at *www.wbenc.org*, the National Minority Supplier Development Council [NMSDC] at *www.nmsdc.org*, or the U.S. Small Business Administration [SBA] at *www.sba.gov*).

Cassandra R. Stanford, CEO of KellyMitchell, a nationwide technology consulting firm that offers a variety of professional services to *Fortune* 1000 clientele, credits her most successful pitch to her WBENC certification:

"I believe my recent success was directly attributable to my joining WBENC's local partner, the WBDC (Women's Business Development Center) and utilizing the tools, events, and connections they offer to women. I hope to show other business women how women are really helping each other through these organizations and, in turn, encourage other women to not only see the value of such organizations, but to participate and make the most of them.

"At KellyMitchell, we recruit project managers and technical experts for clients to supplement their technical staff and to lead/design/complete technology-driven projects. Last year, several of our clients, knowing that we were woman-owned, asked if we were certified. Unfortunately, we were not, mainly because I had the viewpoint that promoting the fact that it was a woman-owned organization would be like accepting a crutch, and that it might take away from the belief that my success has come solely from hard work and perseverance.

"I did some research and contacted WBENC, primarily because they had the largest list of corporations that accepted their certification. I soon found out my thought process was all wrong. I applied for certification and received it in July 2003. The WBDC individual, Debbie Lyall, with whom I worked, encouraged me to attend their annual conference in September and really start utilizing the organization to its potential. Attending that conference really proved how helpful and necessary woman-focused organizations are and ended up being a key in taking my business to the next level. A client I had been targeting, SBC, was in attendance. I was extremely surprised by the amount of corporate participation and the high level representatives that were in attendance. SBC's President of Illinois, Carrie Hightman, spoke at the luncheon and then donated an hour of her time to be auctioned off later that evening. I bid on the auction and ended up winning.

"In January of this year, Ms. Hightman honored our luncheon. During our time together, she was very gracious and I was able to familiarize her with my organization and how we could provide value-added services to SBC. I was working with SBC on a small scale (in a subcontractor relationship) prior to this and was having a difficult time getting in front of the decision-makers to try to become a prime vendor. Ms. Hightman offered to send an e-mail regarding her impression of me and my organization. Shortly following this meeting, I was given an opportunity to meet with the individuals at SBC in charge of purchasing professional services. After meeting them; convincing them I could provide cost-effective, high quality services on a large scale; and obviously, Ms. Hightman's kind words, I was awarded a contract as a Prime Vendor of the national onsite staffing program. This occurred mid-February, and is one of the biggest contracts in IT professional services currently. There are only four of us in this program nationally, so this is a very huge deal! We closed out 2003 with $4.6 million in revenue, and to date, we are already on a run rate of $10 million, if we just stop and coast for the rest of the year—which we won't!—and we will close 2004 out at $15 million.

"My story shows that anything is possible."

Cassandra's story shows that entrepreneurs should use any way they can—including certification—to get a foot in the door of organizations. And, of course, I love her strategy of buying lunch with her dream prospect!

It is important to join organizations in your industry (I, for instance, am a member of the National Speakers Association), but think about it—everyone in the room is potential competition! When you join the industry association of your *clients*, you face virtually no competition. Everyone in the room is a pitchable client! Here are some examples:

- If you are a caterer with one local bank as a client, join a banking association to meet more prospects. It's likely you'll be the only caterer in the crowd.

- If you are a copywriter or editor for educational publications, join a teachers or principals association.

- If you are an independent sales rep for furniture or home wares, join an interior designers association.

- If you are a financial planner targeting high net worth women, join your local Junior League.

I have several CEOs on my prospect list, so I spend $750 a year to be a member of the exclusive CEO Club of Boston. Believe me, that $750 has paid itself back a thousand times with the high-level contacts I've made through this group.

If CEOs and other high-level executives are your target market as well, I highly recommend joining a similar group in your area. With special thanks to Edie Fraser and Best Practices in Corporate Communications (BPCC) for these recommendations, some additional examples across the country include:

- City Club of Cleveland, *www.cityclub.org*.

- City Club of San Diego, *www.cityclubofsandiego.com*.

- The Denver Forum, *www.thedenverforum.com*.

- Detroit Economic Club, *www.econclub.org*.

- Greater Miami Chamber of Commerce, *www.greatermiami.com*.

- World Affairs Council of Philadelphia, *www.wacphila.org*.

I have used association membership to my prospecting advantage on several occasions. One warning: In order not to appear self-serving and "salesy," you may want to volunteer your time or services in order to gain exposure and build credibility *before* you use an association outside of your industry as a prospecting opportunity. Be a giver and a valuable resource, not a taker. For instance, if you are a florist, donate the centerpieces to a large fundraiser before directly marketing your arrangements to association members. Or if you're an IT professional, offer to help develop the association's database. Not sure how to contribute? Join a committee to become active in the association and let them tell you what they need. You'll be gaining exposure and credibility and simultaneously showcasing your talents. Remember, volunteering is a form of marketing.

Here is one story of how this strategy turned out to be essential to several new business pitches I later secured. (In the next chapter I'll go into further detail about how I maintained ongoing personal relationships with the association contacts I mention here.)

In doing my business planning a few years ago, I determined that franchise businesses were a large segment of the small business community (one of my target markets) and I wanted to explore this prospect. I decided to join the International Franchise Association. The following was my action plan:

- Invested more than $1,000 to join IFA. (Like the CEO Club of Boston, this was an investment that ultimately paid enormous dividends.)
- Visited IFA Website and began reading publication.
- Registered to attend IFA National Convention in Orlando.
  - Researched speakers and their backgrounds.
  - Researched IFA leadership. (I assumed they would be at the convention, so I wanted to know as much as possible about them.)
  - Researched member companies and individual members to have a lay of the land before walking into such a new environment.
- Researched the location of the IFA national headquarters and found the office to be in Washington, D.C., where I often travel for business. Made a point to "drop by" the office on my next D.C. trip and introduce myself to several staff members. (Again, in-person relationship building is irreplaceable.)

■ Contacted the IFA's public relations director (I found his name on its Website) and offered to write an article about marketing franchise businesses. Although I had never written for this market before, I sold myself by showing him several article clippings from other association publications and small business magazines.

■ Using the contacts I developed on the IFA staff and with the PR person—and the crucial fact that I was a *paying member* of his organization—I was able to set up a meeting with the IFA's president. Because of the background information I had acquired from the Website, publications, conference, and staff conversations, I knew that they were looking for additional trainers and were interested in setting up a speakers bureau. I focused my proposal on how my providing these services would benefit the IFA's membership.

■ Followed up with the IFA president, continued to visit the office in D.C., and eventually secured a few projects for this influential organization. For instance, the IFA invited me to write articles for its trade publication. One of these articles reconnected me with a past client from Boston who had relocated to San Diego and had become a VP for a large franchising organization. The article led to new business for my company.

■ Because the president of the IFA was pleased with my work, I asked him to recommend me to members of the organization, which he did (see Chapter 9 for more information on endorsement letters). As you can imagine, this has led to several large pitches to major franchising companies.

This entire process took approximately one year from my joining the International Franchise Association to securing a pitch meeting with the IFA president. Over the course of the year, I met dozens of other prospects, added to my portfolio of published articles, learned an enormous amount about franchising, and made new contacts in an industry I had never explored.

If you're visible on a consistent basis, people begin to notice. Remember, it takes time to become an overnight success. What new horizons are waiting for you? What industries can you introduce yourself to? What new business is waiting for your pitch?

Chapter 1 is the essential first step to perfecting your pitch. As Yogi Berra said, "You got to be very careful if you don't know where you're going, because you might not get there." If you want to move ahead with your business and attract new prospects, new clients, and new streams of revenue, you must do the essential background work outlined in this chapter. You have to know *who* you're pitching, *when* you're pitching, *what* you're pitching, and *why* you're pitching. Otherwise, your pitch will always be imperfect and your business will never grow. I encourage you to revisit this opening chapter often—never be complacent about your customer base. You can always expand and be even more successful.

In the next chapter, we will further explore ways for you to "be seen" in your clients' network. So brush your teeth and put on your best suit. It's time to get out there.

Chapter 2

Build Your Reputation and Relationships

As you learned in Chapter 1, building your business isn't about who you know; it's about who knows *you*. So an essential step towards pitching yourself is to build your image in the networks your prospects inhabit. It's time to win friends and influence people.

While we've explored the formal networks such as associations and other professional organizations, some of the most rewarding networking takes place far away from conferences, seminars, and cocktail hours. Remember those stories about CEOs doing business in the men's room? Well, sometimes it's true. (I admit, at some women's business conferences, I've exchanged business cards with the women applying lipstick next to me in the ladies room!)

Reputation 101: See and Be Seen in Your Prospects' Networks

I know you know people. You've participated in associations, and you've researched top prospects and developed a database of contacts. You meet and work with people every day through the general operations of your business, whatever field you're in. But are you getting your message across? Do people remember you? If somebody asked them, would they know what your business has to offer? Put simply, ask yourself whether you have a reputation—a good one.

Nobody wants a negative reputation (for bad customer service, financial mismanagement, or any other poor business practice), but few people work to ensure that they have a *good* reputation. It takes work to build a strong reputation, but the rewards are enormous: When you possess a strong reputation, you will never have to make a cold call again. People will know you by your well-managed reputation, and they will like you before you even begin to tell them how great you are.

The Elements of a Good Reputation

The first person to build your reputation is you. If you want others to say great things about you and your business, you have to start saying it first. Before you can do that, though, you have to develop a succinct statement describing exactly what it is you do so well. Many times in my career, I've had clients and friends say, "Nancy, you are so good at what you do, but I'm not really sure how to explain what you do." I used to laugh awkwardly and say, "I know! No one knows how to describe what I do. It's pretty complicated, but thanks for the compliment."

Not the best strategy, Nance.

Now I have a simple statement I've developed to describe my business—and more importantly, a statement I can teach others to say about me:

> Impression Impact helps companies build and retain the lifetime loyalty of their small business customers through value-added content and training programs designed to help improve the condition of small business clientele.

How do you teach others how to describe you? It's a simple game of repetition. The more people hear you describe yourself (and see your description on your Website, read it in the byline of your articles, and see it in your signature line every time they receive an e-mail), the quicker they will understand what you do and learn how to describe you themselves. Why is this so important? Because you are controlling your image and reputation—an image and reputation that will help you win new business.

It's no coincidence that I named my company Impression Impact—I believe that a strong, consistent reputation is one of the most important assets you possess as a businessperson. And your reputation begins with the words you use to describe yourself. Of course the main driver of your reputation is the quality of work you provide to your clients and customers, but I'm working with the assumption that you are an expert at what you do. So go out there and make sure the world knows how good you are.

1. Elevator Pitch/Introduction

One of the first things I do when I'm working with a small business owner is help him or her write an "elevator pitch." The elevator pitch is a statement to describe yourself in 30 seconds or less, the idea being that if you ever find yourself in an elevator with the client of your dreams, that's about how much time you'll have to convince them that they need to do business with you.

Because you already have your USP from Chapter 1, your elevator pitch should be easy to develop. Here is mine:

"I am the President and CEO of Impression Impact, a company that provides creative marketing consulting services and seminars to small business owners, large corporations, and the franchise market. My biggest clients include Office Depot and the International Franchise Association. I'm also the small business special sections editor for *U.S. News and World Report.*"

Use your USP as the centerpiece of your elevator pitch, then surround it with a few facts that prove your credibility and success record—your evidence. In other words, say what you do, and then prove it, by mentioning that other people have witnessed it.

Advice From an Elevator Expert

Laura Allen, creator of the 15SecondPitch (*www.15secondpitch.com*), focuses on teaching others how to develop their elevator pitches. Here, Laura responds to some common questions about elevator pitches:

Q: Why is an "elevator pitch" so important?

A: An elevator pitch is critical because it is your own personal mission statement. It lets the world know what you do for a living. It also helps you to leave a concise, compelling, and creative voice-mail message for prospects that gets right to the point. There is nothing worse than listening to a stranger ramble on for two minutes on my voice mail and, when those two minutes are up, still not knowing what they are trying to sell to me! If you have a product or service that fills a need for people, they will listen to you. You just need to draw them in and get to the point very quickly.

Q: Why do you recommend 15 seconds for a pitch?

A: If you don't capture the listener's attention in the first 15 seconds of your elevator pitch, you are going to lose his or her attention for good. We live in a world that values anything and everything that is better, faster, and more immediate. You are competing with cell phones, movies, fax machines, TVs, and mass advertising to get a person's attention. The irony is that if you really grab ahold of their imagination in the first 15 seconds, they will usually be willing to spend a lot more than 30 seconds listening to you.

Q: What are the key elements of a good 15SecondPitch?

A: There are four main key elements to every successful 15SecondPitch. They are:

1. Who you are.

2. What you do.

3. Why you are the best at it.

4. Finally—the most important step—your "call to action." In other words, what do you want the listener *to do*, now that he or she has listened to your pitch? For example, are you looking to set up a lunch meeting so that you can win this person's business, or are you looking for an informational interview so you can decide if you want to work for his or her company? Personally, I do not return any phone calls that don't have a clear call to action. "Laura, it was great to meet you at that business networking event," while very flattering, is not a clear call to action, and I won't take the time to return that phone call. A better call to action would

be, "Laura, please give me a call to set up a free 15-minute consultation so that I can tell you how my company can make your life easier." If I believe that this person's product or service can make my life easier, I will invest 15 minutes of my time to learn more.

Another key element of the 15SecondPitch is that you need to choose one and only one niche to focus on. I call it a "pitch for every niche." People don't like to hire a jack-of-all-trades. They want to hire an expert who can solve the problem that they are having today. Small business owners have a tendency to want to sell their product or service to absolutely everyone. If your target customer is the little old lady in Montana on her porch knitting a sweater and the Wall Street tycoon who has just bought another $500-million company, then you are sure to fail. Choose the little old lady *or* the Wall Street tycoon as your target customer. Either segment could be wildly successful.

Salespeople have a different challenge. They need to focus on one key product or service that they are selling. When customers are confronted with too many choices, they will not be able to decide, and you will end up losing the sale. Salespeople need to resist the temptation of telling their prospects about every bell and whistle and, instead, find out what a client's problems are. Once the salesperson understands the prospect's pain, he or she will be in a unique position to prescribe a cure. When you deliver a great solution to someone neatly wrapped in a 15SecondPitch, you make it very quick and easy for them to say yes.

For more information about Laura Allen and her business, visit *www.15secondpitch.com.*

Do you have a unique business that is often hard to describe? Here are some elevator pitches from nontraditional businesses to spark your imagination:

> "I help managers around the world communicate with their employees. For example, I help them draft mission statements and use job descriptions. We recently researched and created the job descriptions for a mushroom farming production supervisor, and drafted the

mission statement for a Middle Eastern coffee bar franchise operation. Our clients improve productivity and job satisfaction for their employees by communicating with them."

—Marilyn Maltby,
Workplace Toolbox,
Austin, Texas

"Hi, I am Tess Bear, Licensed Massage Therapist. I specialize in Deep Swedish, Neuromuscular, Lymph Drainage, and On-Site Chair Massage. Swedish is for general relaxation, Neuromuscular is more specific, and Lymph Drainage is to reduce swelling and detoxify the body. Do you know anyone who has had chronic pain hanging around for more than three weeks? They should see me before taking shots or pills or going under the knife. Relieve your pain and stress with Tess."

—Tess Bear,
Healing Hands,
Memphis, Tennessee

"I've invented a great new gardening tool called WEDGIE, which takes the place of a trowel when planting flower boxes and container gardens. It eliminates digging out dirt! A simple back and forth, side to side motion creates an opening for a plant plug. Each new hole moves the dirt over to fill in around the previous planting. It's fast, it's easy, and there's no mess. Gardeners love it! And it's bright yellow so they don't lose it! It's sold in botanic gardens and garden centers from coast to coast. You can visit my Website at *www.wedgie.biz.*"

—Cookie Wherry,
Wherry Enterprises of Illinois, Inc.,
Chicago, Illinois

Once you've developed your elevator pitch, don't forget to use it! Use it all the time. Practice saying it so you feel natural (and not robotic) when you meet people. I cannot overemphasize the importance of a strong introduction, and your elevator pitch will provide that. First impressions still count for so much, particularly in today's busy times. When you actually meet someone face-to-face rather than by e-mail, voice mail, or phone, you have a golden opportunity to present your entire message, uncut. *You are pitching potential new business every time you meet a new person.* You never know where a new contact may lead, so always put your best image forward and make a lasting impression.

2. Logo

Your visual image is just as important as your verbal image. Even if you are an independent consultant doing business under your name, you need a visual identity—a logo—even if it is as simple as using the same typeface for all of your printed materials.

All too often, I see that someone launches a business and makes the ultimate marketing mistake from the get-go: They create their professional identity on the computer and crank it out to prospects. Newsflash: Everyone else has the same Microsoft Word fonts that you do! You won't stand out as something special if any 9-year-old with a PC can replicate your logo. Especially if you are pitching your business to large companies, you need to look the part. Invest in a logo from a graphic designer who will create a unique design for your business (one of my favorites is Logoworks.com, which will design your logo for as little as $300 or a deluxe version for up to $700). If professionals are out of your price range, hire a graphic design student. Even a typeface logo needs a designer's eye.

Original Logos Designed by LogoWorks

North Shore Cleaning

flying tiger
WEB DESIGN

3. Business Card

My 9-year-old daughter Chloe has business cards. Like Chloe herself, these business cards are whimsical and memorable, and they show her ethnic roots (we had the pleasure of adopting Chloe from China in 1996). Chloe carries her cards in her various handbags, placing some cards in each bag so she will never be without them.

Chloe loves to collect other people's business cards as well as hand out her own. Recently, at the doctor's office, a woman told me about her massage business and handed me her business card. Naturally, I showed it to Chloe for inspection. Chloe noticed that the woman's massage practice was located in Maynard, Massachusetts, where our nanny lives. Chloe insisted on taking a stack of the woman's cards so she could distribute them to our nanny and her friends and family in Maynard. Chloe is a brilliant networker and understands that business cards are the most essential marketing tool in business.

Yes, business cards are *that* important. If there's only one marketing item that you can afford, make it a business card. And make it a great one. The business card is your second line of contact with prospects and clients. It's the part of you that you leave behind after you meet someone. Ideally, it will end up in your prospects' Rolodexes where it will trigger their memory of meeting you next time they're in need of your services.

Don't scrimp when you invest in business cards. With so many inexpensive printers and online resources, there is no excuse for not having a high-quality business card. Opt for the highest stock paper and print quality and the most professional graphics you possibly can. Your professionally designed logo will go to waste if it appears on a flimsy business card. Remember, every time you hand people your business card, you are giving them a little piece of your reputation, so make sure your card reflects the quality impression you want to project.

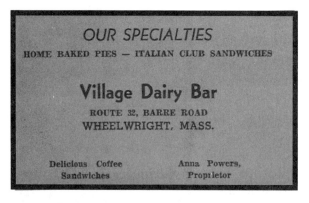

When you think of what to put on your business cards, you may want to think further than your business name and contact information. Some people include information about their businesses as well. Depending on your industry, this can be a good strategy. In my office I keep a framed copy of my grandmother's business card from the 1950s. She and my grandfather owned a dairy bar in Wheelwright, Massachusetts. I came across the card a few years ago when I was deep into my consulting business. I was amazed at the good business instincts of my grandmother. Years before "unique selling propositions," meta-tag searches, and the information superhighway, my grandmother was a whiz at effective marketing. The card listed her USP right there in clear, concise language.

What I love about my grandmother's business card is that you didn't even have to meet my grandmother or visit her business to get a good impression. The card is professional, it's impressive, and it tells you everything you need to know. What does your business card say about you? Does it add to your reputation or detract from it?

While you're thinking about what to put on your business card, consider investing in a CD-ROM business card. These have become increasingly popular, especially among high-tech professionals. When a prospect looks at your card on his or her computer, it will link them directly to your Website. They can also print out your contact information. While I like the cutting-edge element of having a CD-ROM card, I recommend that you do not rely solely on a CD-ROM card. Some people may not react well to it, so you'll want traditional business cards as well.

4. Promotional Kit

I have a question for you. How many brochures do I have to stand on to screw in a lightbulb? About 5,000—it took one gigantic box of brochures to replace my basement light! I used fewer than 500 of those brochures before I finally had the heart to dump them. That is the extent of the usefulness of a brochure. Instead of printing a brochure for your business, opt for a promotional kit instead.

Brochures are a wonderful boost to the old ego ("Come, take a look at my brochure!"), but they will not help you build a strong reputation over time. In fact, I believe that brochures are the worst possible investment you can make in your business for three reasons. A bold statement, yes, but here is my reasoning:

1. Brochures are obsolete almost the moment they come off the press. Think about how much your business changes day-to-day and week-to-week, with new clients, new offerings, or even a new e-mail address.

2. Brochures speak only about you and nothing about what you can do for your prospects.

3. Brochures feel generic and give a prospect no compelling reason at all to utilize your talents.

Sure, the brochure is the most common type of promotional material, but it's also the most useless, especially for newer businesses that are still evolving. A far better option is the promotional kit. It is flexible and can easily be customized for prospects, clients, and the press.

A promotional kit generally consists of a high-quality two-pocket folder that holds informational pieces about your business. To avoid the 8th-grade book report look, use high quality paper for your printed materials inside the folder, and paste a label with your logo to the front. For an even more professional appearance, you can have your logo printed right on the folder. The color of the folder should match the colors you use to identify your business in your logo and on your business cards. It's all about consistency.

The items inside your promotional folder should reflect the strong reputation you want to have in the marketplace. Include:

- **Biography:** This is like a resume, but written in the third person, in paragraph form. Don't be modest. This should read as though your mother wrote it.

- **History of your company:** This should contain a description of the qualities that make your company unique, as well as any personal stories about how you decided to start the business. For instance, if you're a third generation cobbler, include this fact, because it shows longevity, it has a family business feel to it, and it separates you from the pack because it has reader interest and appeal.

- **Press release:** This can be about a new product or service, or it can be a statement of your position on an issue related to your industry or clients. If your views veer from traditional thinking, you are more likely to attract the attention of the media. Other ways to grab attention in a press release are to be timely and piggyback off the news. If you own a limousine company, use the press release to announce that you will offer free transportation on prom night as a way to show your concern with the safety of the teenagers in your community.

Sample Press Release #1

For: Signature Faces, Inc. 114 Wilmington Road, Burlington, MA 01803

Contact: Chris Vasiliadis, 781-750-8350 or chrisv@signaturefaces.com

FOR IMMEDIATE RELEASE

BURLINGTON RESIDENT STARTS NEW BUSINESS, SIGNATURE FACES, INC., TO TEACH CLIENTS MAKEUP APPLICATION IN THEIR HOMES

Burlington, MA—For some women, properly applying makeup is a challenge. They don't know what colors work for them, and where or how to apply makeup to best enhance their features. Further, they'd rather not have their makeup applied in public or experience the hard sell: a frequent occurrence in department stores. In addition, they don't want to pay for parking in the city, or they live too far from places that have quality makeup artists on staff. Signature Faces, Inc., opened for business on May 1st, with a goal of alleviating many of these headaches by bringing makeup services directly to client homes in Eastern Massachusetts.

In just the first month of business, President & Makeup Artist Chris Vasiliadis has been a busy entrepreneur. Her business has not only served clients in their homes, but has sold gift certificates for Mother's Day, donated makeup services for underprivileged women supported by the YWCA of Cambridge, and applied makeup for the models at the New England Women Business Owners (NEWBO) Spring fashion show. Vasiliadis also spoke on and demonstrated Confident Beauty for Today's Businesswomen for the Women in Business Connection (WIBC).

Before Signature Faces, Vasiliadis spent the past 14 years in high tech roles, with the last three years as a makeup artist in her spare time. However, last summer's economic downturn encouraged her to turn her "fun job" into profits. "Getting laid off, not finding high tech work, then receiving that last unemployment check gave me the push I needed to follow my passion for makeup and launch my own business."

Vasiliadis believes every woman is capable of expressing her unique beauty. "Like many skills, makeup application can be easy and fun, once you learn some how tos. When I work with a client, I take many factors into account, including coloring, features and lifestyle. I truly believe makeup is an extension of a woman's personality. Plus, similar to our wardrobe, hair and social interaction, the face we put forward speaks volumes about our style."

Prior to and during a makeup lesson, Vasiliadis uses key questions to grasp her client's needs, and collaborates with the client to design their "signature face" and makeup routine. She uses products from her own kit plus a client's supply, and makes recommendations on what to keep or toss.

A recent client, Adelaide Aitken, had this feedback after her lesson, "I always thought it would take at least 30 minutes to be made up properly, but Chris showed me a few basics that can be done in a few minutes. Thanks to her...for transforming this duckling into a swan."

Besides performing services in the client's home, Signature Faces also conducts consults in client workplaces, and applies makeup for brides and their wedding parties on site. Clients have also booked makeup sessions before an important meeting, job interview or evening out. For more information on services and fees, contact Signature Faces at 781-750-8350, or visit the company website at www.signaturefaces.com.

Sample Press Release #2

For Immediate Release
June 18, 2004

Contact: Ayana Glaze, Principal
(770) 997-3286
Toll free 877-276-3056
ayana@prmoxie.com

MOM RUNS COMPANIES' PUBLIC IMAGE AND NEWS IN "PAJAMA" PR

At the alarm clock's chimes, Ayana Glaze wipes sleep from her eyes, climbs out of bed, and completes her morning ablutions. In all of two minutes she has begun and ended her morning commute to work. In one swoop she rounds the corner to her home office. Still in pajamas, she checks her schedule book, sharp and on the job as a virtual public relations advisor.

Glaze is the principal owner of PRogressive Moxie. She is just one on the crest of an emerging trend on the virtual business horizon—virtual public relations.

Glaze, who began a freelance writing service in 2001, began to redefine her business in 2002 after learning she was pregnant. Internet research led her to a 1998 report by the US Bureau of Labor Statistics. The study predicted the public relations field to be one of the fastest growing fields of the decade

"My determination to succeed illuminated this as an opportunity to turn my public relations expertise, diverse writing skills and creative energy into a home-based business," says Glaze.

She joined the Yahoo group Small Agency PR Pros and Ryze and began to network with others in her field. It wasn't long before Glaze recognized the flexibility that a career as a virtual public relations advisor offered.

"This virtual career path allows me to spend time with my husband and kids, cook dinner, do dishes and still build a successful business," boasts Glaze. "Who wouldn't be happy with that?"

Since taking her business virtual, Glaze says she has served clients across the US and Canada. She now offers extended hours to meet the needs of her global clients.

"My office is open from 9am to 9pm," says Glaze. "I try to offer this flexibility because I want my clients to know that I am there for them when they are working no matter where they are located."

About Virtual Public Relations Advisors

A virtual public relations advisor is an independent PR professional who assists clients via fax, e-mail and phone from the comfort of their home offices. They are of significant benefit to small business owners and independent professionals because of their affordable fee schedules, which tend to be significantly lower than established agencies. Services provided by virtual public relations advisors include public relations writing, media list development, strategic planning, copywriting, internet marketing, media and internet research, counseling and training.

About Ayana Glaze

Ayana Glaze is the principal owner of PRogressive Moxie where she provides an array of public relations services. She received formal communications and public relations training from her alma mater, Georgia Southern University. Her articles on public relations and publicity include "Four Reasons to Send Photos to the Media," "Eight Ways to Recycle a Press Release" and "How to Create a Media Kit Using What You've Got on Hand." She provides public relations tips via her weekly newsletter, *PR Boost*, and has developed **Trumpet Sounders**, a series of small business public relations seminars. Learn more about PRogressive Moxie at www.prmoxie.com, or contact Ayana via e-mail at ayana@prmoxie.com or by calling her toll free at 877-276-3056.

- **List of services:** This list needs to be clear, succinct, and easy to read. Mention *results* that your clients or prospects will receive from your product or service, rather than benefits or features.

Sample List of Services #1

With eighteen years in the business, MIXED MEDIA prides itself on good contacts and diligent follow-up that enables our independent clientele a shot at the level of public awareness that is often only achieved by the majors.

Objectives:

Increase public and media awareness of the client, products, and persona, emphasizing media awareness of the artist's recent CD release.

Schedule:

Mixed Media contracts begin upon approval of a proposal, and media campaigns can be geared towards national, regional, and local segments as well as on-line press. Initial in-market activity can coincide with the press release targeted to all appropriate newspapers (regional weeklies/ dailies), radio (commercial/college/internet/network) and television/video programs.

Publicity:

To raise general awareness, an initial mailing can be sent to national magazines, specialty magazines, as well as general interest publications (i.e. *People*, *Time*, and *Newsweek*), prestige national newspapers such as *USA Today*, *New York Times*, and *Wall Street Journal*, and regional newspapers. Goals are to obtain critical reviews, mentions, and feature articles with as much photo and graphic reprinting of client's materials as possible.

To raise tour awareness, we prefer itineraries at least six weeks prior to appearances and begin press promotion four weeks in advance of each date. We intensely penetrate each local market along the tour as well as keep selected national publications, trades, and directories informed. We draw from a continually updated database of 6000+ newspapers, free-lancers, periodicals, internet sites and are in regular contact with most of their entertainment and music review editors.

Rates:

Our publicity services are billed at the competitive rate of $95 per hour for targets and follow-up, with lower rates for mailing fulfillment, faxing and other "bulk" duties. Retainer fees for long-term (6 month) contracts are negotiable.

Usually a publicity campaign includes a written press release, follow up and expenses (postage, mailers, faxes, long distance calls). The labels provide the promotional materials (press kits, one sheets, photos) and we administer the mailing from here.

Reports:

Detailed progress reports are provided monthly with invoice. This enables us to keep an eye on the costs and assess progress/budgets. We offer different strategies to suit your budget.

MIXED MEDIA   20 Lockmere Road   Cranston RI 02910
401.942.8025

Sample List of Services #2

The following list of services offered is from Chameleon Interiors, available online at *www.chameleon-interiors.com/pages/659042/index.htm.*

Services Offered

Inspirational Room Designs.

We will help you design favorite spaces—from a child's bedroom, a family room, a dining room—whatever you are looking for. We are here to create a complete decorating plan for you, taking into account your lifestyle and passions. From fabrics to furniture, window treatments to floor plans—we can take the burden, and mystery, out of all the decisions both big and small. Take advantage of our trade only accounts—and discounts—with some of the biggest names in the design industry—for that one of a kind look that reflects your personality in its best light. We offer our first meeting (approx 30–45 minutes) at no charge to get to know one another and determine scope of project. After the first meeting, design fee is $100 per hour. Per room design fee is determined by scope of project.

Color Your World.

Sick and tired of all that "builder" white? Have an open floor plan that needs definition? Want a change but are stymied by the literally millions of color choices?

Chameleon Interiors offers personalized color consultations. We come prepared with an armload of color chips and a passion for luxurious color combinations. Together, we will find the perfect color palette to bring your home to life. Typically, this is a 3–5 hour consultation per floor and can be done on site or off. Design/consultation fees are $100 per hour.

Stylish Window Treatments.

Chameleon Interiors will create the perfect window treatments. Fabrics, trims and styles will be married to create one of a kind originals. We work with only the highest quality materials and the best custom drapery makers in the area. Created just for you. Design fee is $100 per hour if not part of a larger design plan; total fee depends on number and variation of windows in room, but generally 2–4 hours per room. Design fee is deductible against final custom window treatment total when purchased through Chameleon Interiors.

Framed artwork.

Chameleon Interiors has partnered with Art Select to offer a complete collection of framed art prints and photographs to complement your interior décor.

One Day Decorating/Staging Homes for Sale.

Need a quick pick-me-up? Selling your house and want it to look its best? Call Chameleon Interiors. In a day, we will come in and do a makeover with what you have! No need for big budgets here. Let our expertise in floor and space planning and a fresh eye bring out the best in your space. As an added bonus, we will prepare a write-up of additional suggestions should you get inspired to make further changes. Fee is $300 per room. Each room is estimated to take 3 hours.

Personal shopping for your home.

You are a busy person. You get dizzy looking at all the colors and product choices out there. You hate spending your weekends shopping. You could use a personal shopper! Hiring a decorator is both a time and money saver. Looking for that special dining room set or perfect sofa? Have an idea what you want, but want to find the best prices in town? Chameleon Interiors can do the legwork for you by researching vendors, using our trade relationships to get the best prices and offering solutions for your decorating dilemmas. Shopping service fees are $100 per hour.

Designer Originals.

Linda offers her designer originals for your home: made to order and one of a kind, created expressly for you with luxurious fabrics, exquisite trims and unique designs. Pillows range from $120–$300; table linens, runners and toppers from $100–$300; throws and duvet covers from $150–$500.

Home Office Design and Organization.

Working at home provides some wonderful benefits, but it also poses some interesting challenges. How your space works for you can be the difference between whether you feel more stress or more joy in working out of your home. More than 15 million people in the United States work at home at least one day a week. Whether telecommuting or running your own business or household, you can't afford to be losing time or money each day because your workspace is not conducive to your needs. Chameleon Interiors is partnering with Sharon L. Fisher of COME TO ORDER!, a professional organizing service, to offer this exciting new design package. Our combination of expertise can provide you with some simple strategies to maintain an efficient workspace and make your space a pleasant and productive environment to be in. Coming soon! Fees to be determined.

- **Client testimonials:** Testimonials are the biggest reputation-builder of all. Your best marketing tool is the quality of your work. When a client gives you a compliment, thank him or her and ask permission to use the comment in your marketing materials. Most freely agree, but then it's up to you to follow up. You might want to speed up the process by writing the testimonial yourself and getting your client's approval.

- **List of references with full contact information:** Your references should be clients. Including these in your promotional materials demonstrates self-confidence. This gives you instant credibility, because it allows the prospect to feel comfortable contacting a client or past client directly, without tipping you off to the fact. Interestingly enough, people seldom call references that are listed this way.

- **Professional photograph:** This can be a headshot or an action shot of you at work. To make sure you look your best, consult with someone you trust on your appearance, including clothing and accessories. You may even consider hiring a professional to do your hair and makeup. You'll want to keep your picture for about four years, so make sure it reflects the image you want to project.

- **Reprints of articles:** Include copies of articles you have written or articles in which you have been featured or quoted. Be sure to arrange these neatly and on nice paper, giving the reader the feel that this is something of value. I lay out my reprints on glossy or heavy paper stock and have them printed professionally rather than photocopied. These make great direct mail pieces to prospects and clients. Unless you've written the article yourself and retain ownership, you should get written permission from the publication to reprint it. State this fact on the reprint by including the line: "Reprinted with permission of [*publication name*]."

- **Company newsletter (if you produce one):** Remember to make your newsletter informative, not just a sales piece. Often a newsletter will naturally double as a marketing piece if the content has value to the reader. Include small bits of information that are easy to digest, such as a letter from the president, a feature story, press coverage you have received recently, "hot tips," and a client profile. You may also want to include an order form for your products or services.

■ **Question-and-answer interview:** This is particularly good for industries or products that aren't easily explained. By posing each question and giving complete responses, you ensure that your readers understand your business. This is a useful tool for soliciting media attention, as well.

Sample Q & A

The following list of questions and answers is from the LogoWorks Website at *www.logoworks.com/Logo-design-questions.html*.

Q: Why should I choose LogoWorks to create a custom logo?

- Quality—LogoWorks' designers are the same designers creating top quality logos for corporations that spend thousands of dollars on their logos.

- Price—For only $265 you can have a corporate image that will rival established, larger corporations.

- Efficiency—You will see your initial compositions in 72 hours (3 business days).

Q: Can LogoWorks design custom business cards too?

Yes. LogoWorks offers a business stationery design package that will leverage the unique features of your new custom logo and corporate image. The package is priced at $199 and LogoWorks will help you find a local printer that can provide high-quality, affordable color printing. If you buy the stationery with the Gold or Platinum packages, it is discounted $50.00.

Q: How much does it cost to get a custom logo and/or business stationery designed?

There are three logo packages, and a stationery package available:

- Silver package: $265 (4–6 original compositions, 2 revision steps)

- Gold package: $385 (6–8 original compositions, Unlimited revisions)

- Platinum Package: $549 (10 original compositions, Unlimited revisions)

- Business Stationery package: $199, includes 2 complete sets of business stationery from which to choose (business cards, letterhead, #10 envelope). Purchased upfront as part of the Gold Corporate ID or Platinum Coporate ID it is discounted $50.00.

Q: Which package should I choose?

This depends mainly on the time you have available, your preferences in reviewing designs, and your budget. If you think you are fairly selective, and want to have more initial logo designs to review, the Platinum package will be better. You will see at least 10 initial compositions, and you have as many revision cycles as you need to make sure you get all of your adjustments made.

If you are in a hurry and have a tighter budget, then the Gold or the Silver package might be a better option.

Q: Is all of the work handled via the Internet?

Yes. LogoWorks is able to provide quality logo design services work because all interaction occurs over the Internet. Projects are started online and the compositions are displayed on your personal project page when they are ready. Logo design specialists are also available via online chat, email, and by toll free phone at 800.210.7650.

Q: Why do I need a company logo?

A professional corporate image can do many things to improve your business. For example:

1. Your business image, and specifically your logo, will have much to do with how your customers think and feel about your business.

2. Quality logos give your business an immediate air of professionalism. Even if your business is new or less established, a customer will often give the benefit of doubt to a company that looks professional.

3. Every business eventually competes with others. A unique and professional logo will help your customers distinguish your products and services and help them remember who you are.

4. Not only will a professional image help you with your customers, it might also help attract key employees.

Q: How will I be able to use my logo?

LogoWorks will post your original artwork on our website where you will be able to access it for download. In addition, LogoWorks will send you a CD with various file formats. You can take this CD to any service provider and they will be able to use your logo as directed by you.

Q: What if I am not satisfied with the work?

We are confident that your design team at LogoWorks will meet or exceed your expectations. If after the first round of logo design concepts you are not satisfied with the work, we will refund your payment, less a $50.00 service fee.

We take pride in the quality of our work and encourage you to review our customers' comments about their LogoWorks experience.

Q: Who can I talk to if I have additional questions?

Logo Specialists are ready to answer your questions through a variety of channels:

1. Email: send questions to support@logoworks.com
2. Online chat: click here to chat with a logo specialist online (M-F, 7:00AM-6:00PM MST)
3. Toll free: 800.210.7650 (M-F, 7:00AM-6:00PM MST)

Not all of the items listed here are appropriate to include in your promotional kit for all prospects. For instance, if you're mailing the package to a prospective client, you may want to remove the press release and photos of a competitor you may have worked with in the past. But that's the advantage of the promotional kit—it easily adapts to your needs. So before you invest in a brochure, consider the promotional kit. No matter how attractively designed, your brochure is stagnant, and a successful company is anything but.

5. Website

Yes, you need a Website. No matter what your business, a Website proves your credibility and confirms your professional existence. Your Website is really your online promotional kit. It needs to explain who you are, what you do, and what other people have said about you. Make sure it looks professional and matches the visual identity you have created with your logo and promotional kit. And don't forget to include photos of yourself—then anyone who visits your Website will recognize you when you meet in person.

You don't need to go overboard, building enormous Macromedia Flash graphics and Amazon.com-level transaction capabilities. If you are a technology consultant or Web designer, this is important. But if you are a cosmetics sales rep, accountant, marketing consultant, dry cleaner, or any other non-IT professional, you don't need a whiz-bang site.

There are, however, some things all Websites really need to have. You want to make sure that you have all contact information at the bottom of every page. Make it very easy for someone to be able to contact you. If you don't have your phone number, fax number, and e-mail address at the bottom of every page, it may be difficult—nothing is more frustrating to me, when I go to a Website and want to contact that company or that person, than going to "Contact us" and not being able to pick up the phone and call them directly. I don't like to be forced to submit something via e-mail because they haven't given their information out. You want to make sure all of that is very easily accessible on your Website. The annoyance of one or two unwanted calls is worth the call you receive from a potential new client who has found your phone number on your Website!

Knowing how to write copy that sells (or how to hire a copywriter!) can greatly improve the effectiveness of your Website. I also think it's great to have really good, "meaty" content on your Website, so there will be a reason for people to stay on your site (the "sticky" factor), and for people to believe there is a good reason for them to return to your site in the future.

Finally, consider using autoresponders, implementing an e-commerce function to your site, and employing a tell-a-friend program, if appropriate to your business. A great resource is *www.1shoppingcart.com*.

Verge Promotional Marketing (*www.vergepromos.com/idea.html*) includes on its Website a unique feature for prospects: a page that the Verge Website refers to as an "Idea Center," which includes a detailed feedback form. The following example shows the information that is included on the online form.

Your project is always our priority. This is a great opportunity for you to experience how we work with you to achieve your goals, and how unique our ideas are in comparison to our competitors.

Take a minute to fill out our quick "ideas on demand" form, and we will be in touch with you within 24 to 48 hours (or if you are in a rush situation, let us know and you will hear from us even sooner!).

By filling out this form, not only will you receive free recommendations from our marketing experts, but if you use Verge for the project, your set-up/digitizing fees will be FREE*!

*Offer applies only to the first order placed with Verge Promotional Marketing, Inc.

Contact Info:

Company Name: _____ *

Type of Company: _____

Contact Name: _____ *

Job Title: _____

Phone: _____ *

Fax: _____

Email: _____ *

Address 1: _____

Address 2: _____

State / Province: _____

Zip: _____ *

Identify your current premium/promotional needs:

Please check all that apply:

Upcoming event ☐

Employee incentives ☐

Upcoming trade show ☐

Direct mailing ☐

Corporate gifts ☐

Sales call giveaways ☐

Public relations mailing/editor gifts ☐

Online custom company store ☐

Other ☐

Please give a brief explanation of your initiative(s) and any other information you would like to provide in the box below:

Quantity needed: _____

Estimated Budget: _____

Event Date: _____ mm/dd/yy

Desired date for
receipt of
merchandise: _____ mm/dd/yy

Another Website example illustrates an excellent way to create a Website for businesses that provide more than one service or reach different client bases. Jane Pollak is both an artist who sells her work and a professional speaker and business coach for other creative professionals. The homepage of Jane's Website, *www.janepollak.com*, makes it possible for each audience to easily find relevant information for its needs. At the same time, by combining both "halves" of her business on the homepage, Jane markets both services to clients who may only know about one.

6. Camera

Huh? What does a camera have to do with a good reputation? The importance of the camera returns us to the concept of creating a strong visual identity to match your strong verbal identity. Think about it—which is more powerful: telling people you met Oprah Winfrey or showing them a photograph of Oprah shaking your hand? I keep a camera with me at all times and always take a photo when I meet people in my industry—speakers at conferences, colleagues, clients, and so on. You'd better believe I have a framed photo of Bruce Nelson standing with his arm around my shoulder outside of the restaurant where we had our $1,050 lunch!

Always get photos of yourself giving a speech and presenting in front of large groups, as well. I recommend investing in a digital camera so you can automatically download your photos onto the computer and directly onto your Website.

As you hone your verbal and visual image, you will ensure that the great work that you do is seen, understood, and appreciated by those who view your materials before they view

Nancy Michaels with Bruce Nelson.

your products or services. Make sure that your online, offline, and off-the-cuff reputation is working for you, not against you.

Identify the Industry Leaders in Your Prospects' Fields: Learn From the Best and Practice, Practice, Practice

When I have small business clients who are stuck for an idea—for a Website, logo, new product name, speech topic, anything—I often recommend they look to those businesses they admire most for inspiration. (Inspiration, mind you, not plagiarism!)

If you want to do business with IBM or compete against Ralph Lauren, your image and professionalism have to match theirs. Even if you don't have the same multimillion-dollar advertising budget or team of publicists, you can still learn from their business practices and apply them to your own endeavors. Ultimately, when you pitch your top prospects, you will need to demonstrate that you can "play in the big leagues," so it's wise to study the rules of their game.

Let's go back to our database and think about those people we included because we admire them and dream of meeting them someday.

Now that you are confident with your product or service, your elevator pitch, and the reputation you are projecting through your image on paper and in person, it's time to get out there and introduce yourself.

There is no question that meeting important people in your industry can help when you pitch new business. Friends who are highly regarded in the business world can be very valuable. A few years ago, I identified one of my dream friends, Nell Merlino, and set about making her acquaintance.

Nell Merlino, besides being a fabulous overall woman, is the founder of Take Our Daughters to Work Day, a very successful concept she sold to the Ms. Foundation for Women. When I decided that I wanted to develop a nonprofit organization related to my work with Office Depot, I immediately identified Nell as someone I wanted to meet. Nell is now a friend and advisor to me. Here is how it happened:

One of my seniormost contacts at Office Depot suggested that I contact Nell, a member of the Office Depot Women's Advisory Board, to explore my nonprofit idea. Based on this recommendation, I immediately researched Nell—her professional background, personal interests, media coverage, business affiliations, and nonprofit commitments. I learned that in a few months, Nell would be speaking at the Women ~ Business ~ Spirituality Conference in New York City. I immediately registered to attend. In the meantime, I continued to read articles about Nell and Take Our Daughters to Work Day. Rather than cold-call her and pitch myself based on the Office Depot contact's recommendation, I waited until I would have the opportunity to prove to Nell that I was interested in what she had to say, and was willing to take the time to hear her speak and meet her in person.

At the conference, I found out where Nell was speaking and attended her session. I waited until the end of the session to approach her (knowing she would not have the time or desire to talk before her presentation) and then introduced myself, using my elevator pitch and explaining that I was a huge fan of the Take Our Daughters project and that a colleague from Office Depot had recommended that Nell and I connect. I said I would love to sit with her at lunch to chat further and perhaps access some of her expertise. She agreed.

Many people make the mistake of using networking as a way of "taking" from other people. It really is the exact opposite—it's about giving, first and foremost. I chose to give Nell my support for her seminar at this conference, and then I told her how we were connected. Even though I had a personal referral to meet her, I didn't expect anything. I wanted our connection to be natural, and it was and still is. We had a nice conversation at lunch that first day and have since stayed in contact and developed a friendship and a professional alliance.

I asked Nell why she agreed to have lunch with me at that conference and why she maintained contact with me. She told me that many people solicit her help and her Rolodex of contacts, but they don't try to connect with her personally. "Business is about win-win situations and I want to work with people who will support and help me, too." Even at the highest levels of business, personal relationships are key. Having Nell as a friend and supporter has taught me much and enriched my business, as well as my life, in ways that a single, out-of-the blue networking phone call never would have.

While it's important to develop and maintain personal relationships with top people in your and your prospects' fields, it's also possible to reach out to many people at once. Even the smallest of small business owners can reach out to top industry players. How? Create an event worthy of their attendance.

One of my favorite marketing/contact-building ideas for small business clients is to throw a *trend theme party*. I borrowed this strategy from a real estate agency where I had one of my first jobs. It was in the early 1990s, one of the worst climates for commercial real estate in the New England market in decades. In addition to traditional advertising in the local real estate journal, we knew we needed to keep communication going with existing clients.

The company decided to host a series of "market overviews" at the prestigious Meridien Hotel in Boston. We hosted breakfast seminars (breakfast is cheaper than lunch!) for our high-end clients and prospects to give them the "insider's" lowdown on the real estate market. By providing them with quality information in a quality setting, we demonstrated our expertise and our professionalism without giving a sales pitch. We were building relationships with prospects, and existing clients.

The market overviews allowed us to keep the conversation going with people who were often losing a lot of money. As the market began to turn, we had already built a successful following for the breakfasts and these events became an important venue for attracting and retaining clients.

When I had my own business years later, I applied this idea to my own circumstances by hosting a focus group at the Boston Adult Education Center. I invited clients, prospects, and leaders of the small business consulting industry to attend a breakfast event (remember our mantra—breakfast is cheap!) to offer their opinions and ideas on certain small business issues of the day. I was able to use the event to demonstrate my expertise and facilitating skills to an important group of people while gathering valuable feedback for my consulting and seminars.

I am always surprised when strangers—particularly those who are high-level professionals—attend an event I host. When I ask what drew them to my events, they often cite the subject matter; if you offer high-quality, *relevant* content that no one else is offering, people will arrive. They also cite my reputation. "I checked out your Website and saw some of the articles about you, so I knew you were legitimate," they say. Don't be afraid to host an event and invite big players in your field and your prospects' industries. If you host a strong event, they will come.

A favorite story of mine involves New York real estate entrepreneur Barbara Corcoran. She wrote a book about her fantastic success but didn't quite know how to promote it, so she decided to host a luncheon to introduce herself to potential book reviewers. She knew that if she was able to introduce herself in person and make an impression, they would consider her book more seriously than if they simply received a generic review copy in the mail. It worked. Barbara's book was featured in dozens of publications during its first month on the market, as well as on *Good Morning America* and the *Today Show*.

Think about your own knowledge and expertise. What are the trends in your field that others would like to know about? What timely information can you offer? When you host a "must attend" event, you efficiently and effectively demonstrate your value to clients and prospects. And remember: Make it breakfast.

Send a Press Release to Show Your Smarts!

In addition to creating theme events to develop and display your expertise, be sure to send a press release as well. Following is one of my favorite examples of an effective informational press release, from The Institute for Luxury Home Marketing, another group trying to reach the competitive real estate community.

FOR IMMEDIATE RELEASE

Contact: Anthony Armstrong

The Institute for Luxury Home Marketing

BOOM IN LUXURY HOME MARKET EVIDENCED IN GROWTH OF THE INSTITUTE FOR LUXURY HOME MARKETING

Increased Competition in Luxury Market Results in Agent Demand for Training

Dallas, TX (March 12, 2003) –The Institute for Luxury Home Marketing recently celebrated a significant milestone when it surpassed its 1600-member mark a full year ahead of original projections. This rapid growth, when combined with recent studies, serves as an important indicator that real estate agents are hurriedly moving into the expanding luxury home market.

According to a recent report by the Harvard University Joint Center for Housing Studies, the number of "million-dollar" homes in the last decade grew 150 percent more than the total number of U.S. homeowners. Luxury, condos, co-ops, and secondary residences were not included, indicating that the true growth rate of "million-dollar" homes is much higher.

This increase in the number of luxury homes, combined with the recent record pace of home sales, is an attractive prospect that has resulted in a dramatic increase in the number of new real estate agents. In response, many agents are seeking out the less-populated territory of luxury real estate.

The difficulty that agents are finding, though, is how to differentiate themselves in an increasingly crowded marketplace. Many are turning to the distinctive value of designations and specialized training, such as that offered by The Institute for Luxury Home Marketing, an international organization providing training, marketing tools, and a luxury home marketing designation for agents who meet specific performance standards in the high priced market.

David Cole, a real estate agent with Prudential Gore Range Properties, has worked in the upscale Vail / Beaver Creek market for over 30 years. Over the past decade, Cole has noticed a significant increase in the number of real estate agents in his county: "We are way over-populated, with over 600 Realtors® in a county whose permanent population is less than 45,000. Realtors® who have an edge on the market get the majority of the business, while others seem to get what's left."

Like many other agents looking to stand out, Cole recognized the increase in the number of luxury homes and sought out The Institute's training and certification program.

"Back in the early nineties," Cole continued, "we started to see development of spec homes valued at up to a million, but now we are seeing spec homes worth 7–10 million. I recently moved my office into Beaver Creek, so I'm hoping [the training and certification] will help me further the luxury market here."

"The competitive market which David Cole talks about is consistent with what's happening nationally," agrees Institute founder and President Laurie Moore-Moore. "With one Realtor® for every 78 U.S. home-owning households, it's easy to understand why differentiation is a key to success. Savvy agents recognize they must have skills over and above those of the competition and must be able to communicate to the consumer that they are unique and better able to meet affluent buyers' and sellers' needs. As a result, our training has been in demand, as have our marketing tools."

"Just 14 months after opening our doors," Moore-Moore continued, "we have trained more than 1600 members on four continents, and the demand for our training is growing. We are excited by such a positive response."

About The Institute for Luxury Home Marketing

The Institute for Luxury Home Marketing exists to help real estate professionals around the world provide high quality service to buyers and sellers of luxury properties. Institute members have completed special training to build expertise in the marketing of upscale homes and estates and those who meet performance standards may earn the prestigious Certified Luxury Home Marketing Specialist designation. Information and an international membership list can be found at www.CLHMS.org. Members are also listed on the Wall Street Journal's www.RealEstateJournal.com website.

Surround Yourself With Success: Create an Advisory Board or Mastermind Group

As you hone in on your most important prospects, it's a good idea to try your ideas out on other people first. You don't want to find out from the *Fortune* 500 CEO you've been targeting that your proposal is a little weak in the implementation phase. No. You want a trusted associate to tell you that *first*, so you can tighten things up and *then* bring it to the *Fortune* 500 CEO.

Many independent business people have developed an informal group of advisors—similar to a company's advisory board—to use as an occasional resource when challenges or opportunities arise. I recommend writing down a list of eight to 10 people whose opinions you trust and whose decisions you admire. Include people who are familiar with you and your business (this is not a "who's who" of your industry) and are likely to provide you with honest feedback. Your list may include former colleagues, former bosses, friends, and even your spouse. Your advisory board doesn't meet together as a group, but exists as a supportive network you can tap into when you need to. For instance, you may call a financially experienced member of your advisory board when you are determining a new pricing strategy.

In addition to an advisory board, I highly recommend creating a separate entity that allows you to gain regular knowledge, support, and insight from people *outside* your industry.

This is where the "mastermind" group comes in.

What exactly is a mastermind group and why is it valuable to be part of one? More than 50 years ago, Napoleon Hill, author of *Think and Grow Rich*, discovered a common denominator among the more than 500 powerful and successful people whose experiences he chronicled: Virtually all of them had created networks of people outside their field. He termed these relationships "mastermind alliances"—groups of people who brainstorm and collaborate on projects, who help each other solve problems and develop opportunities, but do not directly compete with one another.

Something my dad said several years ago has always stuck with me: "When choosing a spouse," he advised, "marry someone who will always be an asset to you." This pearl of wisdom remained my benchmark throughout high school and college romances. All I needed to do was ask myself if my current boyfriend was an asset to me. The answer told me whether or not he was "the one." My father's advice is useful in business as well, his point being that we are who we associate with, and our spouses, like it or not, are a reflection of who we are and how we operate in the world. Your partner, both in your personal and your professional life, needs to be a good and complementary fit. As a businessperson, I now use my dad's criteria when evaluating all of my *professional* relationships. No, I don't require everyone I meet to complete an application! However, I do like to associate with people from whom I can learn, share a common interest, have a thought-provoking conversation, and of course, introduce me to others like us. This is the core of the mastermind group mentality.

Groups such as Business Networking International (BNI) are excellent for getting your feet wet in the world of networking. At BNI, attendees introduce themselves and describe what business leads or professional resources they are seeking. While not always personal, it's a great place to hone your elevator pitch and assess your needs. It's also a nice way to realize that you are connected and have contacts, advice, and resources to share, as well. Remember that giving, not receiving, is the essence of good networking.

I am a big fan of these types of groups for all business owners. It serves as a consistent support network to help propel you toward your biggest dreams. If you're not already part of such a group, I highly recommend creating a group of associates that meets regularly for business purposes.

Creating a mastermind group is an excellent way to develop your professional reputation and also gain valuable advice and support. I've participated in two mastermind groups, and aspects of both have been beneficial. According to Mohammed Fathelbab, former director of the Young Entrepreneurs Organization—an organization of mastermind groups for businesses grossing more than $1 million a year—people join forum groups because "they don't have another venue where they can talk openly and honestly with a group of peers in an environment where they won't be judged." Fathelbab is now president of Forum Resources Network, a company based in Alexandria, Virginia, that teaches people how to form and run forum groups. He says, "The most common thing people say is that the forum is a life-changing experience. It provides comfort, self-confidence, and a realization that you're not the only one with these problems. You come away knowing that other people have the same problems and concerns that you do."

When you are sitting in the waiting area, ready to go in to pitch your business to the client of your dreams, won't it be nice to know you have a group of supporters back home who not only vetted your pitch, but who are cheering you on?

Suggestions for Creating a Mastermind Group

☐ The group should consist of like-minded people who share common goals, dreams, and aspirations, but are not competitive with each other's businesses. Find these people through networking, then start to meet on a regular basis with the sole purpose of helping to achieve your individual and collective goals.

☐ Meetings should be regularly scheduled and agreed to by members.

☐ Meetings may be frequent, but not too frequent because that makes it less likely all members will be able to commit and contribute.

☐ Everyone should agree to attend each meeting or suffer "consequences" (for example, pay a fee to the group, be available on a one-on-one basis after the meeting, and so on).

☐ Agree to meet in a private and uninterrupted space (such as a hotel meeting room, conference room, or private room at a restaurant).

☐ Stick to a prepared agenda distributed to all members before the meeting.

☐ Members should be prepared to present to the group and offer advice.

□ Remember to have fun and celebrate your successes! Business is hard enough, so supportive environments can be a haven from the storm.

In Chapter 1 you looked inward, developing your unique selling proposition; identified potential prospects; and increased your networking opportunities by becoming involved with professional associations. In this chapter you've looked outward, solidifying your visual image and reputation, building your visibility in important circles, and surrounding yourself with a professional network of "masterminds." Now it's time to make the big call.

Chapter 3

The Approach: How to Connect With Decision-Makers

No matter how many contacts are in your database, how dedicated your mastermind group is, or how many people visit your Website, the success of your pitch ultimately comes down to a single individual—the decision-maker. This is the person who signs off on your deal, approves your proposal, and signs the first check. The decision-maker holds the key to your successful pitch.

This chapter focuses on how to connect with your decision-maker—in person, at a face-to-face meeting. We'll discuss a plan of attack for reaching the highest-level people at your top prospect company and for getting your name on your decision-maker's calendar. Remember, you don't actually have to *speak* to your top prospect on the telephone to get a meeting. The goal—the Holy Grail—is the meeting itself. I never had a single personal conversation with Bruce Nelson before the day of our lunch meeting, when I pitched him my small business seminars. You'll have plenty of time to talk at the meeting. Remember: *Just get the meeting*.

Get the Meeting You Want

The first rule when making your pitch is to start at the top. This means setting your sights on your dream company and its top-level employees. It's always best to contact the highest person possible at your target company, even if he or she isn't the decision-maker. So, if you have a connection to the CEO or owner, don't even think about calling anyone else. If you can convince the top person at a company that your pitch is worthwhile, he or she will refer you to the right person in the organization and your call will *definitely* be returned. If you don't know the CEO or owner, make your initial contact with the highest-ranked person you can.

This step-by-step guide will show you how to get the right meeting with the right person.

1. Find a Referral

The goal of all of the research and networking we did back in the previous chapters is to make sure you "warm call" your prospect. (As opposed to "cold calling" them, which we all know gets a chilly response.) The best way to warm up a call is to tell the person on the other end of the line that their friend, colleague, or acquaintance recommended that you get in touch. Referrals are golden. If you have developed genuine relationships through networking, mastermind groups, and association activity, you should be able to find a referral to your top prospect. Never be shy about dropping names.

I highly discourage you from calling a company and asking for "the head of marketing" or "the person who makes your outsourcing decisions." I've been an administrative assistant and I can tell you that this is a red flag: "Sales call! Sales call! Send this person to voice mail!"

On that note, part of your research must include confirming the correct pronunciation and spelling of your prospect's name. As one successful entrepreneurial friend told me, "If someone calls and mispronounces my name when they ask for me, it's clear they don't know me or anyone who knows me, so I simply hang up."

Because you are now focused on meeting your top prospect face to face, you'll need to supplement the information you've already collected about this person. If you haven't gathered this information already, now is the time to find out:

- Where exactly is his or her office located? (Note that some CEOs frequently work at alternate locations from the company's headquarters.)

- What are the best restaurants convenient to this office location? (Your local *Zagat* guide is the best source for restaurant research.)

- Does my prospect go out for breakfast, lunch, or dinner meetings (or none of the above)?

- Does this person support a particular charity? In some cases you can offer to donate a certain amount of money to the charity of your prospect's choice in order to "buy" lunch with that person—this is a more personal version of bidding for lunch with a CEO, as I did with Bruce Nelson.

If you are pitching a large corporation, you may want to start with a local branch of the company to build your reputation before approaching the big guns. Pamela Moore of Ice Tubes, Inc. used this strategy extremely effectively with the largest corporation in the country: Wal-Mart.

After attempting to insert ice cubes into her son's sports bottle, Pam realized there must be an easier solution. Rather than a conventional ice cube, why not freeze water into the shape that would fit into a bottle's opening? She hit upon the idea of ice that could readily slip into the mouth of the bottle—an "ice tube."

As with all start-up businesses, the path to success was challenging. Moore had the concept, but bringing it to fruition was another story. Calls to manufacturers and designers went unanswered, but she persevered and found a nearby firm that was willing to work with her in developing the product. The final prototype was a tray of 27 cylinders that produce tubes of ice to fit into the necks of most plastic beverage bottles such as bottled water, bottled soda, and sports drinks.

Bringing the product to market—or pitching the product to retailers such as Wal-Mart—proved an even bigger challenge. After flying to meet with Wal-Mart buyers and being turned down cold, Moore went to her local Wal-Mart store and asked the store's manager to sell her product—which he did. Upon positioning Ice Tubes next to an end aisle of Gatorade, the drinks flew off the shelves, as did Ice Tubes. With that information in hand, Pam proved to Wal-Mart that her product had real sales potential and corporate executives took notice. Today, thanks in part to high volume sales at Wal-Mart, Ice Tubes, Inc., generates revenues of more than $5 million!

2. Send Something First

It's always a good idea to send your promotional kit and a cover letter to your A-list prospect—hopefully the CEO—before making the first phone call. If this person already knows you (through an association, mutual contact, or other means), your envelope will be opened. If he or she doesn't know you, the envelope will still be opened, but likely by an assistant. Either way, this initial contact by mail is unobtrusive and professional. It also gives you a "reason" for your first phone call. You can send this letter by first-class mail or a priority mail service such as FedEx or UPS—it's really up to you. With the ubiquity of priority mail services these days, it doesn't give quite the sense of immediacy it used to.

I recommend sending your promotional kit to your top prospect with a cover letter including:

- How you found this person's name and contact information (name drop!).
- A brief introduction of you and your business.
- A brief explanation of what you are offering and how you can help this person's business.
- Acknowledgment that you will be contacting them shortly.

Your cover letter should be brief and focus primarily on your prospect company and what you can do for it. Think of it as a cover letter that accompanies a resume—the goal is to entice the recipient to read the enclosed information.

Sample Promotional Kit
Cover Letter #1

Top Prospect
Company Inc.
123 Main Street
Anytown, US 12345

Dear Ms. Prospect:

John Doe of XYZ Company suggested that I contact you. John thought you would be interested in my work helping *Fortune* 500 companies to better serve the small business market.

Considering Company Inc.'s new initiative to reach small business owners, I feel that a series of in-store seminars delivered to your customers would be beneficial in building the lifetime value of your customer base. I have attached a press kit for your review.

Ms. Prospect, I will be in your city on May 27 and 28 and would love to meet with you, if you have time in your schedule.

I will follow up with you soon. In the meantime, please do not hesitate to contact me. I can be reached at 781-860-8881 or nmichaels@impressionimpact.com.

I appreciate your time and consideration and look forward to hearing from you soon.

Regards,

Nancy Michaels
President
Impression Impact

Here is a fabulous example of using compelling, newsworthy information in a cover letter. If I were an advertiser wanting to reach women, this letter would surely compel me to find out more from Vicki.

Sample Promotional Kit
Cover Letter #2

Dear Ms Prospect:

Did you know that a crisis is emerging in mass marketing in the financial services industry? You don't have to look very hard to see that it's severe: According to BAI Global, response rates for credit card solicitations have steadily declined from 2.8 percent in 1992 to an all-time low of 0.6 percent in 2000.

Marketers are spending more and more money—and getting less and less in return. Worst of all, this crisis is partially of the marketers' own making. Why? Because for years, financial services companies have spent billions mistakenly chasing younger consumers, a relatively un-affluent, shrinking demographic cohort. At the same time, they've essentially ignored the demographic sweet spot of the market: Baby Boomer women. The mistake is costing marketers billions in lost opportunity.

Why are women truly banks' most important customers? It's because they are the "Chief Purchasing Officer" in over 80% of all households. Here's the data:

- Women handle the checkbook in 85% of households.
- Women carry 76 million credit cards—8 million more than men.
- Women control or influence 67% of household investment decisions.

- Women start 70% of all new businesses.
- Women have sole or joint ownership of 87% of homes, and buy 61% of major home improvement products.
- Women buy 68% of all new cars.

How can your company reach this exploding market? Advertise in *Women's Business*.

Circulated to 25,000 each month, *Women's Business* is the only regional publication guaranteed to reach the influential, high net worth women's market.

Let's set up a meeting in which I can show you how to reach the decision-maker in 80% of all households.

Sincerely,

Vicki Donlan
Publisher

Finally, never forget to use what you've got! If you are a creative professional, use your artistry in your promotional package. If you are a calligrapher, write each address in beautiful lettering. If you are a photographer, include images on the exterior of your envelopes. If you design promotional gifts, send your pitch in a basket. Rose Scharmen, owner of the Cloth Envelope Co., has a very unique product that sells itself: beautiful cloth mailing envelopes. She, of course, sends all of her mailings in her own products and her promotional kit includes lovely samples that the recipient can touch and use. Here is the creative letter Rose sends to prospects:

Cloth Envelope Co.
5581 Trager Rd.
Traverse City, MI 49686

Hi there!

This is your Cloth Envelope talking. I just jumped out of your pile of mail and begged to be opened. You did. Guess what else? You won't throw me away. Wherever you put me, I will remind you of the invitation, announcement, or information I contain. Want to learn more about me? Ask for your free Cloth Envelope Special Events Promotion Kit:

Phone: 231.995.9515
Fax: 231.995.9516
Email: sales@ClothEnvelope.com

Snail mail the address above

And don't forget to visit my Gallery, A Showcase of Ideas, on my Website, *www.ClothEnvelope.com*.

I am USPS approved.

Cloth Envelope Co.'s tagline is "Envelopes That Get Opened." That's the goal we all have, so take a few tips from her creativity and brainstorm ways to entice your prospects to open your mail and learn more about you and your products or services.

In another example, Maggie Melanson, President and CEO of Gimme the Skinny, a low fat catering company in Norwell, Massachusetts, wanted to approach Oprah Winfrey (everyone's dream client!). Maggie asked me for advice, and I recommended that she use her biggest asset—her delicious, healthy food—to reach Oprah and her staff. Maggie agreed immediately and prepared a catered meal for Oprah's magazine staff in New York City. She brought trays of food onto the airline shuttle! Now Maggie is on the *Oprah* magazine radar screen and will likely be interviewed for an upcoming article on healthy treats.

3. Pre-Call Prep

While you are waiting three to five business days for your package to arrive on your prospect's desk (and actually be opened), you can spend your time preparing for your first direct contact. Decide how you will keep track of your calls. Ideally, you should record your phone calls in the same database where you keep your contact information (Best Software ACT! is a great program for this). Other people prefer keeping a handwritten "phone log" so they can scribble notes during phone calls. Either way, keep a record of your phone calls so you never have to wonder, "Did I call Carly Fiorina's office already?"

In your log or database, you will eventually keep track of:

- Date and time of phone call.
- The exact phone number you called (main number or direct line?).
- Whether you reached a voice-mail message or a real person. (If voice mail, what did you say? If a real person such as an assistant, what is the assistant's name?)
- If you need to call back, the date or time recommended by the person to whom you spoke.
- The elements of the phone conversation (if you succeeded in getting through to your prospect).

Sample Telephone Log

With so much phone calling, you need to keep it all straight—when you call, whom you call, and what was accomplished. Dorothy J. Madden, founder of Organize It!, a professional organizing company that helps clients get organized in their offices and homes—and in their home offices—shared her telephone log with me. Dorothy's company mission is "to create solutions for managing her clients' time, space, and information, so they have less stress and more time to do what's most important to them." Sounds good to me!

Dorothy recommends this telephone log system because it is simple, records the necessary information (especially the action required), and can be photocopied and clipped to a clipboard or hole-punched and placed in a colorful binder. But she advises that you make sure both the clipboard and binder are portable and large enough not to get buried on your desk!

TELEPHONE LOG

DATE & TIME	NAME	PHONE NUMBER	MESSAGE	ACTION REQUIRED	DONE

Sample Follow-up Log

Here is an example of a more detailed follow-up log, adapted from the copyrighted form used by Olalah Njenga of Marketing With Ease. Each time she is in communication, or has a "touch," with a contact—by telephone, mail, e-mail, or in person—she uses this form to indicate how she intends to follow up and to write down key information and goals.

MARKETING WITH EASE™

TODAY'S FOLLOW-UP LOG: _____

FOLLOW UP!	
CALL WRITE SEND	WHO:
Contact Information:	
This is touch #:	What do you ultimately want:
What was agreed to/decided at the last touch *(recap of previous touch)*:	
What is the desired outcome of today's touch *(goal of today's touch)*:	
How would you briefly recap today's touch *(setting up the next touch)*:	

4. Determine an Appropriate Meeting Format

At this point, before making a call, decide what kind of meeting you want. With some prospects, it's perfectly acceptable to explain that you are offering a new product or service and would like to set up a meeting to introduce yourself and your offering. In other cases, you'll need to have a few "getting to know you" meetings to show your value and build your credibility before you can make your official pitch. This explains my spending $1,050 to have lunch with Bruce Nelson of Office Depot. With most large corporations, it's likely that you won't actually make a formal business pitch until you've met on multiple occasions.

When thinking about what kind of meeting you want, be sure you can answer these two questions:

1. How can I offer value to my prospect in this first meeting?

2. How can I use this meeting to build a relationship?

Notice that these questions are about what you can do for your prospect and your prospect's company. Keep the focus on their needs, their problems, and their schedule.

If you are less experienced in your business, you may consider requesting an "informational interview," to treat your prospect as an expert resource that may someday be a client. This is a highly recommended strategy for start-up business owners who need to build credibility early on. The "value" for the prospect in an informational interview is that he or she is treated as a valued resource and advisor. If you do choose the informational interview route, be very clear about your intentions and, of course, very appreciative of the prospect's time.

For more advanced businesspeople who are looking for a relationship-building meeting strategy that will fulfill the two questions list previously, I highly recommend the "CEO interview" strategy.

I learned this ingenious strategy from Terri Kabachnick, a very successful consultant and speaker in the retail industry. Terri and I met through the National Speakers Association. Terri's wise advice is to always position yourself as a "partner and problem solver," not as a salesperson. One way to do this is to ask for an "interview," rather than a meeting, with the CEO of your top prospect companies. This is a great strategy for connecting with multiple prospects in a short period of time.

Here is what Terri recommends: Based on your industry expertise and research, develop a research project that will be extremely relevant to these companies. Then call each prospect and explain that you would like to interview your prospect for this research report. Be very specific in your overview of the *results* you will be able to offer from this report (increasing sales in this industry, saving money, and so on). Explain that you would like to ask your prospect five specific questions and it should take approximately 30 to 45 minutes. Be sure to mention that you are also interviewing other companies in the field and will share your findings and recommendations once the research is completed.

The interview strategy is smart for several reasons:

- If you are interviewing someone, you are not talking about yourself. This means that you will learn more about your prospect and understand more about the company's issues and needs. This is valuable data for your future business pitch.

- You have a perfect reason to follow up: to reveal the results of your research. At that future date, you will have an easier time getting a meeting with your prospect because you've already met for the interview. In fact, it's best to set the follow-up date at the end of your interview to ensure that you secure a slot. "Let's set a date so I can present my research to you in person and show you how my findings can help your bottom line" is a great way to close the interview.

- If you do not end up working with the companies you interviewed, you can still use the data for articles, speeches, and other business purposes. Although you may not use the companies' exact names or details, your research helps build your credibility and position you as an expert.

I used the CEO interview strategy to develop a relationship with a retail store that claimed it had an interest in reaching out to women business owners. Weeks before I planned to call this company, I met Mary Cantando, author of *Nine Lives*, a book of interviews with successful women business owners. Mary shared with me the fact that, in researching stores to approach to sell her book, she learned that this particular retail store had only four books on its shelves that were authored by women—four out of 100 books! This was a dismal statistic and seemed, in my opinion, to contradict the company's statement that it supported women in business.

When I called to set up a meeting with my prospect contact at this company, I mentioned that I had some research to share that concerned the store's strategy to reach out to businesswomen. I knew it was unlikely that anyone else had shared this information with the company's top management and I wanted to be a resource to them. I got the meeting.

Perhaps my all-time favorite "get the meeting" story comes from Sara Blakely, who invented Spanx footless body-shaping pantyhose. As Sara explains it on her Website (*www.spanx.com/SarasStory.aspx*):

> "Once I had a perfected prototype in hand, I called the buyer at Neiman Marcus and introduced myself over the phone. I said I had invented a product their customers would not want to live without, and if I could have ten minutes of her time, I would fly to Dallas. She agreed! I put the prototype in a Ziploc bag from my kitchen, threw it in my good-luck red backpack, and was on a plane. During the meeting, I had no shame... I asked her to follow me to the ladies room where I personally showed her the before/after in my cream pants. Three weeks later Spanx was on the shelves of Neiman Marcus! I then called all my friends and begged them to go to Neiman's and make a huge fuss over the product and buy them up. At just the moment I was running out of friends, Spanx caught on and the rest is history. I did the same thing with Saks, Nordstrom, Bloomie's and all my other retailers!"

Not all of us can hold pitch meetings in a ladies room—or use a tag line like Spanx's "Don't worry, we've got your butt covered!" but Sara's story is certainly an inspiration to all!

Think about how you can be a resource to your top prospects, no matter where you are. If they come to trust you as a resource, they are more likely to trust you as a vendor.

5. Get in the Right Frame of Mind

I don't want to make you nervous, but calling your top prospect is a big deal. Don't treat this like any other phone call you'll make during the course of a business day. Here are some tips I've learned over the course of my career:

- **Call when you're feeling positive.** Perhaps the day after you've finished a big project or closed another significant business deal is a good time. If you are worried about money or feeling stressed and anxious, your prospect is likely to hear it in your voice. Be smiling when you call and your positive energy will be contagious.

- **Be in "business mode" when you call.** Sit at your desk, call from a regular phone (not a cell phone that may cut out), sit up straight, and clear away all background noise such as the radio, television, dogs, and children. This is particularly important for businesspeople who work from home. If you are calling Xerox, you need to sound as if you are calling *from* Xerox.

- **Write a mini-script.** I don't recommend *reading* from a script (you'll sound like a telemarketer!), but I do recommend easing your nerves by jotting down some key words or key phrases you'd like to include when you reach your prospect or have to leave a voice-mail message.

6. Be Prepared for the "Ask"

Okay, I lied. Don't be prepared. Be very, very, *very* prepared. Many businesspeople prepare themselves for disappointment but forget to plan for a positive response. If your top prospect says, "Sure, let's set up a meeting," you have to have a plan in mind. Will you invite your prospect out to lunch at a nice restaurant? Will you offer to travel interstate to the prospect's office? Think of all the possible scenarios and prepare accordingly.

In general, you should think of this meeting as an investment and spend accordingly. Do not scrimp by offering to take your prospect to an inexpensive restaurant or balking at the cost of a plane ticket to their location. If you want to meet your top prospect, you need to make it easy for them to meet with you. In other words, do whatever your prospect wants.

If your prospect is a small business owner or sole proprietor, then by all means take him or her out to lunch. Many people with small businesses rarely leave their offices and like to be treated to a meal at their favorite restaurant.

Don't overlook the power of the stomach when it comes to prospects at larger companies (hence your earlier research into your prospect's favorite mealtimes and locations). However, it's often difficult to secure a meal with a *Fortune* 500 CEO. For prospects at larger companies, I recommend the "end time" strategy. I learned this trick from Terri Kabachnick as well. She suggests saying to your prospect or your prospect's assistant, "Let's set up the appointment for 10 to 10:45 a.m." If you suggest a specific end time, your prospect will feel like he or she can "get away" if necessary. The meeting is less of a burden this way.

The upside for you is that this tactic often has the opposite effect: During the meeting, you can keep your eye on the clock and graciously offer to stop your fascinating presentation with a few action-oriented conclusions at the exact scheduled end time. (We'll talk more about pitch presentation content in the next chapter.) Hopefully, your prospect will be intrigued by this point and will invite you to stay a bit longer. This gives you the advantage of being "invited" rather than feeling like you are begging for time. Of course you need to be prepared for the possibility that you'll have extra time to share more information and ideas.

Just remember, do whatever your prospect wants. Make it as easy as possible for your prospect to say yes to a meeting, and prepare, prepare, prepare.

Now you're getting ready to pick up the receiver and press those fateful buttons.

CEOs Don't Answer Their Own Phones: How to Get Through to Busy People
The Assistant

There are few guarantees in life, but this is one: When you finally feel prepared and confident enough to call your top prospect, he or she won't answer the phone. Sometimes you'll get a voice-mail message, but more often than not, you'll speak to an assistant.

An assistant can make or break your chances of securing a meeting, so it's smart to be prepared for a conversation with this important gatekeeper. Most of the senior corporate executives I know have very close relationships with their assistants and trust their judgment enormously. Today, many sole proprietors and small business owners, myself included, employ an assistant as well.

Become as friendly as you can with your prospect's assistant. Do your best to find out the assistant's name before you even make the first call so you can address him or her by name. Often you can find this name by calling the company's main number and asking. Another trick is to call your prospect's voice mail very late at night when no one will be there. Most people's messages include a phrase such as "If I'm not available, please contact my assistant, Megan, at extension 123."

Here is a sample interaction with an assistant, using the CEO interview strategy:

Assistant: "Hello. Top Prospect's office."

You: "Hello. Is Top Prospect in?"

Assistant: "I'm sorry, he's not in. Can I help you?"

You: "Well, maybe you can. Is this Megan?"

Develop rapport with assistant. Acknowledge the assistant's position of influence.

Assistant: "Yes."

You: "Thanks, Megan. This is Nancy Michaels. You may have received the package I sent last week. Mr. Big Name Referral from Mega Important Corporation suggested I call Mr. Prospect to speak or perhaps set up a meeting."

Use a referral name, if you have one, as early in the conversation as possible. Also refer to your written materials, which were likely opened by the assistant.

Assistant: "What is this in reference to?"

You: "I am doing some research in the small business industry and I've been interviewing CEOs for my project. I'm interested in perhaps 20 to 30 minutes of Mr. Prospect's time to conduct the interview. I met with Mr. Big Name Referral last week and he thought Mr. Prospect would be an excellent candidate to interview."

Be very specific in your request.

At this point, the conversation can go in two different directions. The assistant can take you for your word and respect your referral. This might lead to a call back from your prospect or the chance to schedule an interview. If so, congratulations.

On the other hand, you may not have as strong a referral as you think, or the assistant may be more difficult than you anticipated. If this is the case, you'll need to try another tactic:

Assistant: "I'm sorry, Ms. Michaels. Mr. Prospect is too busy for interviews, and he is not accepting any new business pitches right now."

You: "I see. Maybe you can help me, Megan. How do you recommend I approach this? I know how busy his schedule is, but Mr. Big Name Referral highly recommended I call and meet with him to discuss how I can help your company save money based on my research findings so far. Perhaps I can send an e-mail with more detailed information?"

Let the assistant be the expert on your prospect. It's also smart to offer an alternative means of communication such as e-mail.

Assistant: "Well, okay. Why don't you send an e-mail to me and I'll make sure Mr. Prospect receives it."

I have an excellent example of a making-friends-with-the-assistant success story from my own career. I once worked with the CEO of a major corporation on a large program that required his assistant to coordinate a large mailing on my behalf. To thank the assistant when she completed the project, I sent her (and the CEO, of course) a basket of cookies from a bakery in my town. Four years later, this large corporation was hosting an event for business owners, and by the time I found out about it, it was sold out. So I called this assistant to ask if she remembered me and if she might be able to add me to the guest list. She said, "Of course!" and thanked me again for the cookie basket while adding my name to the sold-out event. I'm not sure I would have received such a friendly response had I not sent her the gift! This story again proves how going the extra mile can make a lifetime of difference.

Voice Mail

If you are not able to form such a nice bond with an assistant, it is also possible to reach a CEO or senior person directly, by calling before or after hours. Most assistants work "normal" business hours (ranging from 8 a.m. to 6 p.m.), while most decision-makers work earlier and later. Try calling at off-hours to get through.

This strategy will likely result in reaching your prospect's voice mail. Voice mail provides the opportunity for you to leave a detailed message. Your goal in a voice-mail message is to provide information that leads to another communication. Whenever I leave a message, I *always* say that I will also follow up with an e-mail. It can be difficult to find out the e-mail address of a top corporate executive or government official, but in most cases you can learn this information from a Website or receptionist.

When I sent a promotional kit to eBay CEO Meg Whitman and wanted to follow up with a call, I connected to Ms. Whitman's voice mail. I left this message:

> "Hi, Ms. Whitman. This is Nancy Michaels from Impression Impact. I just left a message with your assistant. I know you are incredibly busy, but Bruce Nelson gave me your name and suggested I contact you about my research on marketing to small business people for increased ROI. I saw the recent article in *Fast Company* magazine about your small business efforts and wanted to contact you right away. I'm overnighting you a package that your assistant should receive tomorrow and I'll also send you an e-mail so it's easier for you to get back to me."

I highly encourage you to use this e-mail follow-up strategy. The majority of people would rather respond by e-mail so they don't feel "on the spot." In this instance, I also referred to a recent *positive* news story. Top executives like to know that their PR efforts are working.

Polite Stalking and Other "Alternative Tactics"

If your best efforts to contact your top prospect by phone and e-mail fail, there are other tactics you can try.

One alternate route is to contact the company's public relations or communications person. The PR department often works closely with the senior decision-makers at a company to ensure that opportunities are not missed. If there is a PR angle to your pitch (such as the potential publication of research you are conducting), the communications department may help you get your foot in the door.

You can also "politely stalk" your top prospect. This strategy is an extension of the tactics you learned in Chapter 2. Show up at events your prospect is attending and make contact. If you can quickly make an impression on your top prospect in person, mention this when you make your phone call. Try to find something memorable to say or give to the person so they recall who you are. One trick is to write a personal note on the back of your business card, mentioning something or someone you have in common ("I'm Bruce Nelson's client—let's talk!" or "UCLA Class of '75—a fellow Kappa!") or that mentions a recent article or tidbit you learned about your prospect's company ("Saw the great *Journal* article—I can help with your new marketing-to-women Website"). *The trick to being memorable is to be specific.*

When you do hand over a business card or chat at a live function, be sure to *ask* if you can contact your prospect. "May I call you on Monday?" will either get you an invitation to make contact (which you can mention to an assistant or on a voice-mail recording) or information about an alternative means of communication. Often a busy person will tell you the best way to make contact ("E-mail is the best way to reach me" or "Call my assistant, Lynn, and tell her we met at the NSA conference"). Follow these directions to the letter!

Another alternative tactic I recently discovered is so simple I can't believe I hadn't heard of it before. I found it in a fantastic free e-zine that I subscribe to: *Idea Site for Business* (*www.ideasiteforbusiness.com*), run by Mary Gillen and Andy Attiliis—a good reminder to subscribe to a variety of free online newsletters, because you never know where or when inspiration may appear. Gillen and Attiliis share the tactic of a financial services saleswoman who targeted physicians as her market but had difficulty setting appointments with her busy prospects. She came up with the wise idea to set up an appointment as a patient with each physician and actually paid for each doctor's time so they would hear her pitch. Using this method, she was able to add several new customers to her client list. Think about your own prospect list—are there any professionals with whom you can buy time if you have trouble reaching them through other methods?

If you're not afraid of more overt tactics, I offer the story of my colleague Jennifer Flynn, who once wanted to target major hotels as clients. She decided to attend a hotel conference to hear a speech by the CEO of Wyndham Hotels, Fred Kleisner. Coincidentally, Jennifer sat next to the CEO of a big public relations firm in Boston. She ended up telling the CEO the story of my buying lunch with Bruce Nelson. The PR person told Jennifer that she *had* to go up and talk to the Wyndham CEO, particularly because his speech referred to Wyndham's commitment to serve businesswomen like Jennifer. So Jennifer took the advice and followed Mr. Kleisner out of the building.

"I have to tell you I am so excited to meet you," she told him. "My colleague Nancy Michaels will pay you $1,050 to have lunch with us."

(Not that Jennifer asked me first, but I'll continue the story....)

He replied, "You don't have to pay me!"

As a follow-up, I wrote a letter referring to the situation, telling the CEO that I hope Jennifer had not scared him, and offered to take him to lunch.

The story does not end there, however. Jennifer tells me that after she went up and talked to Mr. Kleisner, several people at the event suddenly came up to speak to her. They perceived her as knowing the CEO, which made her a desirable person to talk to. In fact, Jennifer later won Best Western as a client, because she met a representative at that very event. All of this happened because Jennifer showed up and took the opportunity to make a personal connection with her dream prospect!

Understand the Capabilities of Everyone on the Team

We started this chapter "at the top," which is a very good place to start. But once you secure the meeting with your top prospect (through direct contact, best friendship with the assistant, an e-mail message response, or some variety of legal stalking), you'll need to begin to learn the roles of other members of the decision-making team. Even if you are pitching a sole proprietor, it's important to understand who else will affect the decision about your pitch, and whether these people will attend the meeting you've scheduled. Even if you are pitching an individual consumer, ask yourself, "Will I be meeting the spouse or children?"

You can uncover some of this information through research and networking, but much of it will not be revealed until you actually meet with your prospect company. It sounds like a dilemma (how can I know the people I need to know before I know who they are?), but it's not. The key is to *be sensitive and inquisitive* about office procedures, policies, organizational charts, and yes, office politics. If you are sensitive to potential issues, egos, and domains of influence, you'll be sure not to step on any toes.

My best advice is to ask these questions openly. As early in the process as possible, once you've secured a meeting, ask your prospect directly, or ask your prospect's assistant the **following** questions:

- Is there anyone else I should contact about a meeting on this topic?
- Will other members of the team be joining us?
- Who else works in this division?
- Who reports to whom?
- What are the internal policies and procedures might I need to know about?

Your goal is to find out as much as you can about anyone involved in making a decision about your pitch. Your research will pay off when you finally meet these very important people face-to-face. Be careful, be honest, and be aware. You can't know everything, but you can do your best to be "in the know."

If you have conducted appropriate research, prepared a business offering that is on-target with your prospect's needs, requested an appropriate meeting format, and acted politely and genuinely with all members of your prospect's team, by now you've gotten the meeting you want—congratulations!

The next chapter will guide you through my essential preparation strategies to ensure that the meeting you've worked so hard to secure will be a resounding success.

Chapter 4

The Only Pre-Meeting Checklist You'll Ever Need

What is the essential first step to take when you hang up the phone call confirming your meeting with your top prospect? Celebrate! Yell "hurrah," pump your fist, call your best friend. Take some time to relax and enjoy your achievement. This is why we're in business—for the moments of excitement and success.

Then, once you've celebrated, get back to work. It's time to prepare for your meeting. Nothing guarantees the success of your meeting like good preparation. You may have the best ideas in the world; you may hit it off immediately with your prospect; but if you're not prepared, the meeting will be just that—a meeting. It won't lead to anything else. In my opinion, 70 to 80 percent of the success of a meeting depends on good preparation. It's likely you'll only have a few weeks to prepare, so I've put together a comprehensive to-do list for you to follow, from the moment you secure the meeting until the day of the meeting itself. Work these action items into your particular timetable for a personalized pre-meeting action plan.

The List

Not all of these action items will apply to every meeting, so follow the steps that make the most sense for your business and opportunity.

Send a Thank-You Note

Write a quick thank-you note to the person with whom you've arranged the meeting. A personal handwritten note is best, but e-mail is
fine as well—particularly if you've interacted with several people in order
to set up the meeting. Keep your note short and sweet.

Review All of Your Current Marketing Materials

Several weeks or months may have passed since you first sent your
press kit to your prospect. Take a moment to review the information
you initially sent out and compare it to your current materials. Has
anything changed? Do any of your materials need updating with new
client information, an improved product offering, or any other
changes?

You should bring copies of your most updated press kit to the pitch
meeting, so start preparing early, in case you need to allow time for
printing or photocopying.

Call Everyone You Know

Now is the time to tap your mastermind group, advisory board, networking groups, association members, and anyone else who may be able
to offer information that will help you to be as prepared as possible for
this meeting. You will want to ask:

- Do you know any of the people I'm about to meet?
- Do you know anything about the company?
- Would you please keep an eye out for information or articles
  about this company? (The more eyes searching on your
  behalf, the better.)
- Is there anything about my business or current product
  offering that you think I may be overlooking or need to work
  on?

Really listen to the comments of your most trusted advisors. Although sometimes it's hard to hear the truth, it's better to hear it from
friends and colleagues than from the prospects you're pitching to!

Play 20 Questions

No matter how much pre-pitch research you've done, it's foolhardy to assume that you know exactly what your prospect wants and needs. It's best to go into your meeting planning to ask a lot of questions. Face-to-face, you can ask all of the questions you couldn't answer through search engines and networking, but it's important to use your pre-pitch research to formulate your questions. For instance, "I read that you are creating a new ad campaign to reach the small-business market. What new products are you developing for that particular market segment?"

Return again to the company's own Website (if they have one), *www.Hoovers.com* (for larger companies), and *www.Google.com* (for smaller companies and individuals), to learn as much as you can about your prospect—and to absorb any new information that has come out since conducting your initial prospect research. *Always confirm that you have the most current information about your prospect.*

The Best Questions:

◪ Explore new developments about your prospect. It's impressive to show that you are on top of new developments and current events.

◪ Allow prospects to talk about their companies or, even better, themselves. People like to talk about their accomplishments and share their opinions.

◪ Provide insight into your prospect's biggest concerns and headaches. What has disappointed them? What has worked well for them in the past? What are their most pressing problems (that you can solve)?

Sales expert Peter Groop, president of Fusion Sales Partners, wrote an article for *Inc.* magazine that has always stuck out in my head. In his article, he points out the most important question to ask: What do your customers want to buy? "Sell what they're buying—not what you're selling," he advises. According to Groop:

> "Sell your firm's products and services and you'll experience modest success. Understand what the customer *wants* to buy—and then meet that need—and you'll experience

tremendous success. Remember—the customer is not buying your firm's machine—they're buying the result which the machine helps to provide."

Wise advice, indeed.

Bring your list of questions and refer to it often. Show your curiosity and desire to understand and respond to your prospect's most pressing needs—not the needs you think they should address.

Design a Clear and Concise Visual Presentation

Always bring a presentation to your prospect meeting. You may not have the opportunity to show every slide or even to show the presentation at all, but it's crucial to bring information about your company and capabilities. I didn't go through my presentation over lunch with Bruce Nelson of Office Depot, but before I left, I gave him a hard copy of the presentation as well as a CD-ROM version so he could pass it on to other members of his team.

Presentations (and the accompanying leave-behind copies) are crucial, but many businesspeople make the mistake of creating presentations that are too long, too boring, or too focused on themselves. Make sure your presentation helps your cause. Here are my do's and don'ts for creating perfectly presentable presentations:

Presentation Materials:

1. *Do* err on the side of creating a shorter presentation rather than a longer one. Less is more. Remember: This meeting is primarily for information-gathering. Your formal proposal will come *after* this meeting, when you can match your skills with your prospect's needs. (My best advice for creating a short presentation is to create as long a presentation as you wish, then show it to at least five people *outside your industry*. Remove any slides that don't hold their interest.)

2. *Do* create professional presentation materials. The beauty of today's technology is that it creates a level playing field for small businesses and independent salespeople. Even the "small guys" can create presentations with impressive visuals and some (but not too much) animation. Not proficient with

technology yourself? Hire a smart high school or college student to help with your graphics—that's what I do and the results (and cost) are fantastic.

3. *Don't* use more than two font types in your presentation. This confuses the eye and draws attention away from your message.

4. *Do* use lighter letters on a dark background. This is more visually appealing than black letters on a plain white background.

5. *Do* bring your own laptop and projector if you plan to give a PowerPoint presentation. Don't rely on your prospect to provide you with any technology. Burn your presentation onto a CD-ROM as well, in case you experience any problems with the presentation document on your laptop.

6. *Do* take a lesson in Microsoft PowerPoint, so you know how to use this technology. It's inexcusable to tell your prospect that you don't know how to work the equipment to show your own presentation materials.

7. *Do* have a backup plan. Bring printed copies of your presentation (more than you think you may need, in case additional people attend your meeting), so everyone in the room can follow along and take notes. Because you can't guarantee the size of the room or know whether your laptop may crash five minutes before your presentation, hard copies are a must for backup as well.

Presentation Content:

1. *Do* customize your presentation with your prospect's company logo. Show them that this presentation is about *them,* not you.

2. *Do* offer brief background information about your company and yourself. Reference your press kit, but work under the assumption that they may not have seen it.

3. *Do* briefly share your personal story. This is the chance to build a relationship with your prospect; they want to know the person with whom they may invest their time and money.

Include a professional head shot in your presentation for an even stronger personal touch. Again, make sure the photograph in your presentation is consistent with the photograph in your press kit. Consistency = professionalism!

4. *Don't* write out exactly what you are planning to say; this is the biggest mistake presenters make. Never read the words exactly as they are printed on the screen. This is the surest way to put your audience to sleep. You know your stuff! Use visual images to enhance the words you are planning to say.

5. *Do* use numbers, statistics, and diagrams. Impressive numbers are often more compelling than words when it comes to a business pitch. This is crucial if you know that key financial managers will be in the room during your meeting.

6. *Don't* outline every project you've ever done for each of your 20 clients. Instead, use testimonials to build your case. A single glowing sentence from each client, testifying to your value (again, use numbers), will be sufficiently impressive. And remember to include your clients' company logos with their testimonials. This is especially important if you've completed work for well-known companies in your industry—brand names really stand out in a presentation. (Be sure to obtain approval from your current or former clients before using their names in your presentation.)

7. *Do* include relevant press clippings about you and/or your business. These clippings may work best as attachments to your hard-copy presentation materials, but be sure to include them to demonstrate your high profile.

8. *Do* include a list of references containing all contact information. Be prepared with this information *before* your prospect asks for it. This shows confidence and planning on you part. Again, confirm with your references that this is okay.

9. *Do* show your presentation to as many people as possible to catch typos, redundancies, or grammatical errors. These are inexcusable in a pitch presentation (or any presentation, for that matter).

When you are satisfied that your presentation is ready, back it up on your system and burn it onto a CD-ROM for your files. Stephanie Cohen and Hayley Byer, managing directors of Verge Promotional Marketing in New York City, make CDs of their presentation to distribute to all meeting attendees (bring extras just in case!) as well. They always create custom CD labels with the prospect's logo rather than distributing plain CDs. According to Stephanie and Hayley, prospects often comment on this extra touch that shows Verge's attention to detail—an important quality to find in a promotional marketing firm.

Rehearse

Practice your presentation in front of anyone and everyone you can. Rehearse in front of your mastermind group, colleagues, or family members for feedback on presentation style and content. It's always a good idea to videotape yourself as well. No better format exists for analyzing yourself. When you are rehearsing, look for:

- Presentation content: Is it meaty? Interesting? High-level?
- Presentation style: Are you talking too fast? Too slow? Do you suffer from the "um," "err," or "you know" tics?
- Time: Is it too long or short?
- Appearance: Does your hair fall into your face? Do you slouch? What are you doing with your hands?

Plan Your Appearance

Appearance matters. No matter how strong your presentation materials, content, client list, or financial results, your prospect will draw certain conclusions based on how you look and act. You've worked too hard to get to this point to lose business because of a messy or unprofessional appearance. Don't let ill-fitting clothes or an outlandish tie or earrings detract from your message.

While you shouldn't spend thousands of dollars every time you pitch new business, it is worth it to invest in professional items such as a leather portfolio or briefcase and a classic pen. It's all part of the pitch—remember, you are selling yourself.

Other aspects of your appearance and accessories to consider:

- ◪ Suit: Always, always, always err on the side of too conservative when it comes to the clothes you wear to a meeting with your prospect. And try on everything a week or two before the meeting—the morning of your big day is not the time to learn that your favorite suit no longer fits!

- ◪ Haircut: Don't get a drastic haircut the day before your meeting, but do make sure your hair is neat and looks professional.

- ◪ Accessories: Be careful of the brands you associate with. It's a familiar warning, but an important one: Don't bring an IBM laptop to pitch your business to Dell. Don't carry a leather handbag when you pitch an animal rights nonprofit.

- ◪ Grooming: If you like to have a manicure, your hair styled, or other professional grooming, plan accordingly. Work these appointments into your calendar at a time when you won't feel too stressed to take the time for the appointment.

How do you know if your appearance fits the bill? Put together your entire outfit and accessories and show it to someone who will give you a truly honest opinion. Who can you trust to not hold back on what they really think? I don't know about you, but for me, it's my mother-in-law.

Check Your Credit Card Balance

Remember, if you are taking your prospect (and possibly his or her entire team) to breakfast, lunch, or dinner, it's on you. So are all of your travel expenses to get to your prospect's place of business. Chalk all of this up to the cost of doing business, but do plan ahead so you can buy a cheap ticket!

Confirm Your Appointment

Call a few days before your meeting to confirm the time and location of your appointment. Often this communication can take place through your prospect's assistant, which has the added bonus of providing another opportunity for you to bond with this ever-important gatekeeper.

Other than confirming your meeting, try not to contact your prospect between the time you make the appointment and the appointment itself. You don't want to seem like a pest. However, if you read of a major development at the company, by all means, send a note.

Plan to Arrive Early

If it weren't somewhat insane, I would probably sleep in my car outside my prospect's office building the night before an important meeting, just to guarantee I'll be on time! Of course this is ridiculous, but do plan to arrive early for your meeting. You are pitching your business, so there is absolutely no excuse for being late. You may need to sit in your parked car for a few minutes until the appointed time, but anything is better than running late and sweating in traffic!

Don't Forget Your Confidence

A positive, composed demeanor is essential for any pitch meeting. A firm handshake ("Two pumps, and let go," advises Diane Darling of Effective Networking, Inc.) and a genuine smile are the perfect opening move.

Ladies and gentlemen, it is now time to let the pitch begin.

Section

II

During: What to Do With Your 15 Minutes of Fame

Chapter 5

Pitch Your Prospect's Socks Off

Welcome to the big day, the moment of truth: pitch day. Take a deep breath, check yourself in the mirror (no breakfast residue in your teeth, no runs in your nylons or stains on your tie), and put a smile on your face. It's go time.

Prepare an Agenda

When preparing an agenda for any meeting, think about the outcomes you want to achieve, and *then* determine the discussion topics you will need to cover, in order to achieve these outcomes. Ask yourself:

- Do I want to get my foot in the door with a basic introduction, do I want to secure a small project to begin working with this prospect, or do I want to win a large amount of business?

- How much time will I realistically have in this meeting? Always assume you will receive *less* time than you would like, so you don't run the risk of not getting to the items on your agenda.

I generally write the agenda at the last moment possible, when my presentation is complete and I have read the week's news (in case any major change has occurred in the company, the economy, or the world that might affect our work together).

An agenda shows immediately that you have a plan for the meeting and you will not waste time rambling. It helps you set the tone of being prepared and in control.

Keep the agenda as simple and straightforward as possible. Here are some tips for creating a winning pitch-meeting agenda:

- Print the agenda on your letterhead, which of course matches the business card you will give to each attendee and the visual materials you will present. Consistency, always!

- Title and date the agenda, so everyone at the meeting has a written record for future reference. When listing your company name and your prospect's company names in the title, always feature your prospect's name first, to show your "client first" attitude.

- Limit the agenda to one page. A multi-page agenda will immediately alienate your listeners and cause flashbacks to the daunting syllabus for Russian Literature 101.

- Include no more than five or six bullet-point topics, and keep them short and simple. An agenda should be easy to scan and make the reader interested to hear more information about each topic.

- "Introductions" is a foolproof first agenda item for a meeting with a new prospect or a meeting involving people you have never met face-to-face. Introductions break the ice, allow you to glimpse the personality of each attendee, and help calm any last-minute nerves.

AGENDA
ABC Company & Impression Impact
May 24, 2004

- Introductions
- Exploration of ABC Company's Needs
- Impression Impact Presentation Services
- Q & A
- Next Steps

- The last item on your agenda should refer to "next steps" or "follow up." Including this item on your agenda will ensure you never leave a pitch meeting without establishing the client's expectations for your follow-up.

In your mind, each agenda item should correspond to an amount of time you plan to spend on that topic. This will help you control the timing of the meeting. Remember, if you asked for 30 minutes, do your very best to stick to that and keep the meeting on schedule. Your prospect will respect that you are considerate of their time. Let *them* be the ones to lengthen the meeting beyond the allotted time.

For virtual businesses, such as professional coaches or virtual assistants, your pitch meeting, by necessity, may take place by telephone rather than in person. I am very impressed by the comprehensive way Fabienne Fredrickson, who calls herself a Client Attraction Coach, informs potential clients about her services and what they can expect to learn before they sign up for Fabienne's coaching. This following example is the e-mail prospects receive after showing an interest in her services and requesting a consultation. It is designed so that she can collect all the info she needs to be prepared for the conversation and to make her pitch.

Hello,

Thanks so much for reaching out.... I'm happy that we connected today, and I look forward to chatting with you.

Here's what I propose to help us make our time on the phone even more efficient and valuable by focusing on YOU:

1) If you haven't yet, please read the "Interview with Fabienne" sheet on *www.clientattraction.com/interview.html*. It's a very comprehensive walk-through of the many questions you might have, with detailed answers for each. **Please read this in its entirety.**

2) Read the Client Testimonials on *www.clientattraction.com/testimonials.html*. They'll give you a very clear idea on what my clients have gotten from this System.

3) Please send me the answers to the following questions over **e-mail, prior to our call**:

* How many clients do you have?

* How many do you want/need?

* How much is each new client worth to you, in terms of revenue (on average)?

* What are you doing currently to market your business?

* What obstacles, challenges, and struggles do you regularly come up against?

* What would you like to see happening 12 months from today (realistic goals, but a bit of a stretch)?

Please call me at 203-595-0068 at the time of our appointment. Can't wait to hear about your situation and see if I can help.

One more thing: just send me a quick reply to let me know that you've received this.

Thanks

Fabienne

Get your free checklist "151 Ways to Attract All The Clients You Need" by sending an e-mail to: ClientAttraction-On@lists.webvalence.com.

Sign up for free teleseminars here: *http://www.clientattraction.com/events_classes.shtml*

If you need more clients, you'll want to visit: *http://www.ClientAttraction.com* for free articles, compelling client testimonials and info on private coaching.

Fabienne Fredrickson, The Client Attraction Expert, Creator of "The Client Attraction System™"

203-595-0068; 866-RAINMAKER (toll free) Fabienne@ClientAttraction.com

(See Page 136 for Fabienne's post-call communication.)

A Note About Technology

If possible, ask for access to the room where you'll be making your pitch beforehand, so you can set up your equipment prior to the meeting. Most receptionists or assistants will help you coordinate this, if you arrive early enough and the room is available. This can help you save crucial minutes better spent pitching than plugging in.

The Pitcher's Mantra

Baseball pitchers talk about getting into "the zone" when they walk onto the playing field. Get into the zone by repeating the following "rules" to yourself before you pitch any new client:

- I will create a win-win situation.
- I always have my client's best interest at heart.
- I will be flexible and listen to the needs of my prospect rather than jamming my agenda down their throats.
- I will encourage open communication and listen more than I speak.
- I will not badmouth my competitors (there is no advantage to this—and you never know; they may be pitching 10 minutes after you leave!).
- I will stick to the allotted time frame, unless the prospect extends the meeting.
- I can handle anything that happens in this meeting.

Your mind creates your reality, so go in with positive thoughts and your energy will be contagious.

The First 5 Minutes

No matter what your agenda may say, I can't help but refer to the first five minutes of a pitch meeting as "make or break time." We all know that first impressions are crucial, so do your very best to start your meeting on the right foot, even if you are anxious.

First, be sure to greet everyone in the room with a strong, firm handshake and direct eye contact. Exchange business cards as early into the meeting as possible so you can keep track of everyone at the table and his or her title and department.

If you need to set up a projector, do this as quickly as possible and try to chat while plugging in your equipment. Avoid awkward silences.

Follow the prospect's lead regarding seating. If you are pitching with another person from your company or a business partner, split up instead of sitting next to each other. Commingle with the people you are pitching, to create a team atmosphere, rather than sit on one side of a table and create a sense of two teams competing against one another. You want to be next to the people you are pitching.

Pitching Over a Meal

While most of the tips in this chapter apply to any pitch meeting, some differences do exist when you pitch over a meal in a boardroom or a restaurant. Generally, you will know in advance if a meal will be involved in your pitch, but sometimes the prospect may surprise you. Here are some guidelines to follow, based on etiquette and common sense:

☐ Don't select a meal that takes too long (or is very messy) to eat. Avoid spaghetti, ribs, shellfish in the shell, and so on.

☐ Never order alcohol, no matter what your prospect orders.

☐ Be polite to restaurant staff or the servers at the prospect company. Remember that your every move is being observed, so treat everyone with equal consideration.

☐ Follow your prospect's lead regarding when to begin talking business. If they make small talk, make small talk. If they start to talk business the minute you sit down, follow suit. However, if the meal is progressing and no business has been broached, politely begin to raise some of your prepared questions.

☐ If you are meeting at a restaurant, pick up the check, no matter what. It is your meeting, and the results may lead to financial reward for you, so paying for lunch is the right thing to do. You should also tip generously, as the restaurant may be a frequent choice for your prospect and he or she will find out if your tip was less than impressive. Consider it all the cost of doing business.

When your prospects introduce themselves, particularly any contacts you have not met previously, try to get a sense of each person's position and responsibilities. You can then cater parts of your subsequent presentation to the people most affected.

Following the prospects' introductions, I always begin by briefly thanking my prospect for taking the time to meet with me. Then I launch into my opening spiel:

"As you might recall, one of my clients is Jane Smith at XYZ Company and she thought you would be interested in hearing how I saved her money and provided a better service. Before I get too much into the nitty-gritty of providing some of my ideas for your organization, I would like to find out a little more about you and what you're looking to achieve. I'd like to know how I can best help you."

This should open up a dialogue. During the dialogue, consider asking the following key questions to guide the conversation in the direction that will be most helpful to you:

- What is your biggest challenge right now?
- If you could change one thing in your organization/ department/product/service/life what would it be?
- What is keeping you up at night?
- What have been your best (and worst) vendor experiences?

While you are asking questions, always take notes. This makes people feel important and helps you document everything that takes place. You can later reference particular comments or ideas in your thank-you note, follow-up materials, and proposal.

No matter what your allotted meeting time, do not interrupt a good conversation to show your presentation. Establishing rapport and making your prospect feel important, valued, and listened to is more important than showing your presentation, no matter how fantastic you think it is. You can always use your printed presentation as a leave-behind. Remember—and this is a good rule of thumb for personal interactions as well: *People generally care more about what they have to say than what you have to say.*

On the other hand, your prospects may not engage in conversation at all. As someone who loves to chat, I find this quite strange! However, I have come to understand that some businesspeople, especially those who may be listening to dozens of new business pitches, prefer to sit back and passively listen to a presentation. If you sense this is the case with your prospects, shorten the question/dialogue component of your meeting and launch into your prepared remarks.

Responding to Challenges

The last chapter talked you through the creation of a killer visual presentation, but as we all know, your prepared presentation is only one element of a strong pitch. The live, unscripted component of a pitch meeting can veer in any direction (positive or negative), and is equally important to your end goal of sealing the deal.

The following are some common situations that arise in a pitch meeting and my best advice for turning each potential challenge into an opportunity to further demonstrate your strengths.

■ **A meeting attendee begins to challenge you or your business.**

Ah, the contrarians. While some companies purposely play good cop/bad cop in a meeting, sometimes you will be faced with someone who is in a bad mood or simply argumentative by nature. No matter what the reason, do not let a challenging person affect your confidence or "ruin" your pitch.

The most important reaction is to acknowledge the person challenging you. Whether or not the person's questions or complaints are legitimate, acknowledge the person's comments with a comment such as, "I'd love to get more information about that. I will get back to you with a more specific answer."

If the challenger contradicts your facts, numbers, or beliefs, a good strategy is to ask for more information. For instance, "Hmm, that differs from my research. From what source is your information? May I e-mail you for more information about that?"

No matter what, you cannot get defensive. Keep your cool and move on as quickly as possible.

While we are on the subject, now is a good time to discuss the importance of knowing your numbers. You *must* be prepared to discuss financial matters in detail. You must be able to explain how the client company will see a return on investment, how you will track results, and what benchmarks you will reach. Overall, the most important financial question to answer is: What value do I bring to the table?

If you are not comfortable remembering numbers in detail, bring notes, a calculator, or your key financial staff person—whatever makes you feel comfortable. It is never, ever acceptable for the CEO of any size business not to be able to defend his or her financial projections. Yes, math counts.

■ **They ask about price before you understand the scope of their needs.** In today's competitive economy, cost is a paramount concern to all businesses. What do you do if a prospect asks about price first and foremost? A good first move is to turn the question around and ask the prospect about the company's budget. Try to determine what range they are expecting to pay. Although their numbers may be lower than their actual budget, it will help you to have a ballpark figure.

If your prospect is unwilling to disclose any of the company's budgetary information, here is a response that may help advance the conversation:

"Well, price is a concern for every consumer in the market-place today. To come up with an accurate price I need to come up with a formal plan for you. Perhaps we can schedule a follow-up meeting for me to come back to deliver a proposal with detailed costs. I'm sure we can negotiate a price structure that makes sense for both of us."

If the prospect absolutely insists on a number, consider describing the cost structure of a similar project, but try to describe costs within a range, rather than providing exact dollar figures.

- **They question your experience/expertise.**

Prospects may challenge your experience for a number of reasons, ranging from a fear of working with a small business, to a negative experience working with a contractor in the past, to general worry or insecurity. While your presentation should include some examples of your work and professional references, it is always smart to have more information in your briefcase or, at the very least, organized in your brain. You must be prepared to present your credentials and successes with detailed examples and evidence. Your backup evidence may include:

- A list of references who have agreed to speak on your behalf. If possible, provide the prospect with references who have something in common with them—industry, city, company size, and so forth.

- Written client testimonial letters.

- A list of key accomplishments from various client projects or product lines. Remember, while references and testimonials are always subjective, no one can argue with hard data.

- Your resume, including education, work experience, and a list of accomplishments from your business. Yes, even entrepreneurs need resumes!

- **They ask why you are no longer working with a past client.**

This is a tricky one, similar to when a recruiter asks a job seeker why he or she left an earlier position. Tell the truth as much as possible, but keep your answer short and sweet. There is no need to launch into a long story about a former client who didn't pay his bills, or a project that went haywire. You should anticipate that this question might arise, so be prepared with a concise answer, such as, "We completed the agreed-upon order and moving forward didn't make good business sense for either of us" or, "There were personnel changes that led to the selection of a new vendor." Under no circumstances should you lie or misrepresent the situation. Your prospect can easily check your story, and lying in a pitch meeting is a guaranteed way to lose the deal.

■ **They question whether you, as a sole proprietor or small business owner, are big enough to work with their company.**

Many corporate professionals need a bit of convincing before working with a small or even medium-sized business. I recommend a two-pronged approach to respond to such a concern:

◪ Demonstrate your strong focus on serving your clients. Make it clear that you will be able to service any and all of their needs, and if you are limited in any area, you are willing to invest the resources to improve your offering. For instance, you can mention trusted subcontractors or associates with whom you can work if necessary. If you have successfully worked with subcontractors or associates on past projects, by all means, give specific examples.

◪ Highlight the advantages of a big company doing business with a small guy. Here are some of my favorite arguments in favor of the small guy:

6 Advantages of Working With a Small Business or Independent Agent/Consultant:

1. **Responsiveness**: Small businesses and independent consultants can respond quickly and turn on a dime in case of strategic or directional changes.

2. **Smaller overhead**: Because they do not have to support a huge corporation, small businesses can charge smaller fees to provide high quality service.

3. **Network of experts**: Most small business owners focus on their core competency and then access specialists as needed. Small business owners will assemble the best team possible to serve their customers' needs.

4. **Quick decision-making**: Small business owners and independent consultants make their own decisions and don't need to work through a lengthy corporate approval process. Corporate clients like to know they are always working with the boss.

5. **Innovation and creativity**: Small business owners are experienced in outside-the-box thinking and devising creative solutions. Big companies that rely on consensus decision-making often lack this innovation.

6. **Customized service**: It is no secret that a large corporate contract is extremely valuable to a small business owner. You don't need to say, "I will worship you!" But you can explain that the corporate business will be your highest priority.

■ **The meeting deteriorates into disaster.**

There is no nice way to say it. Some meetings simply stink. Even if you have done all of your homework and think you have found your ideal client, face-to-face meetings can prove otherwise. If you do face an antagonistic client and it seems impossible to make a connection or convince them of your expertise, then perhaps the relationship is not meant to be. If a client is difficult at the first pitch meeting, chances are that this is a sign of things to come. As Maya Angelou said, "When someone shows you who they are, believe them." You have a right to choose your clients, just as much as they have a right to choose you.

However, bad pitches can be a good experience. If you walk out of a pitch meeting and decide against further pursuing that company, think about their competitors. You have already researched the industry, the company, and probably the competitors, so take your newfound expertise across the street, where your product or service may better fit.

Even if you end up pursuing clients in an entirely different industry, do not look at an unsuccessful pitch as a failure. At the very least, you will be better prepared for a future pitch of any kind. Chalk it all up to experience.

Discussing Next Steps

Ideally, the meeting will be a winner and your time will end with a discussion of follow-up plans. Here are some tips for ensuring that your follow-up plan will lead in the right direction:

- *Don't* leave without making your major point. Meetings can progress in a variety of directions (sometimes the results are better than expected!), and you should always be flexible and as accommodating as possible, but do not leave a pitch meeting feeling as though the prospect does not know what you are capable of delivering. It is okay to take a minute or two at the end of a meeting to remind the prospect of your offering.

- *Do* briefly recap the main points you gathered at the meeting, to show that you have been listening and to make sure your impressions are correct. "So, what I've heard you say is...."

- *Do* ask what the prospect would like the next steps to be, then set a time frame for responding. Ideally, ask to set up a meeting at which you can present your customized recommendations based on the information you gathered at the pitch meeting.

- *Don't* overpromise. It is tempting, especially at the end of a good meeting, to proclaim that you will single-handedly transform the business of your prospect and do everything under the sun to please them. While enthusiasm and confidence are both great, do not make the mistake of promising more than you can deliver. Even though nothing is in writing yet, be careful to manage your prospect's expectations. Be positive and energetic, but be realistic.

◪ *Don't* try to close on the spot. It is very rare that a deal, especially a large one, will be decided based on one meeting. The best outcome of a pitch meeting is to feel that you have built rapport, created trust, and learned enough about the prospect's needs to know how you can best fulfill them. Don't jump the gun.

Congratulations! Walking out of a good pitch meeting is one of the highlights of a business owner's life. Now the strategic work begins. The next chapter will help you create a win-win proposal that your prospect won't be able to resist.

Chapter 6

Submit an Outstanding Proposal

Remember the advice from the last chapter to listen more than you talk during a pitch meeting? Now is your chance to prove that you really heard your potential client. In this chapter, you will implement your client's comments and respond to their needs by creating a completely tailored follow-up proposal. Your proposal will include details on the program you are pitching, benefits of hiring you, the expected cost, a timeline, stories of satisfied customers, your bio, relevant media you've been featured in, and references.

Ideally, you will present this follow-up proposal in person. This will give you more information and makes it harder for them to say no. By presenting in person, you will get immediate reaction and can respond to any challenges rather than waiting weeks to submit a revised proposal.

Show Them That You Heard Them

Your first order of business is to find out how your prospect would like you to format your proposal. I recommend e-mailing your prospect after sending a formal thank-you note for the pitch meeting. The benefit of e-mail is that you do not intrude on the prospect's time, and you have a written record of his or her recommendations that you can refer back to in the future. If necessary, you can follow up with a phone call during which you should take copious notes. Be sure to ask about the following factors that will affect the format, content, and presentation of your written proposal:

The Format

■ **Length:** If your prospect requests a one-page outline of recommendations and costs, do not send a 20-page wire-bound proposal. Do not give your prospect more work! If you send a proposal that is too long, it may never be read.

Your post-pitch proposal should always be appropriate to the tone and format of your business.

Remember Fabienne Fredrickson, the Client Attraction Coach whose pre-call e-mail I shared in Chapter 5? Her post-call follow-up is appropriate to her virtual coaching business. Rather than sending a letter or proposal, she outlines the client's needs in an e-mail message following their first consultation. Here is an examples she has used with a client. I particularly like her last sentence:

Hi [prospect's name],

I enjoyed talking with you this week. It's very clear to me that you have everything it takes to make your professional goals happen. It's really great to see that. As I understand it, these are some of the things you would like to work on, based on our conversation:

* Take your practice "full-time" by doubling your client base from the current 5-10 clients a week to 15-20 clients a week.

* Start taking on telephone clients to expand your market beyond New York (and make more money).

* Select from and focus on one or two of your current "many ideas" as to not dilute your efforts.

* Promote yourself and your services to get new clients quickly.

* Increase your number of group workshops.

* Get better at marketing them and filling them.

* Create "price packages" or programs so that clients stay with you longer and you make more money.

* Learn how to get new private clients from workshops (existing and future).

* Make more money than you currently make with current clients (raise rates!).

* Create a rate sheet to make it easier for clients to sign up with you.

* Start selling your workbooks.

* Get weekly goals, a practical action plan.

* Stay accountable.

These all sound feasible and are very exciting goals!

[*prospect's name*], I'm ready to begin tackling them with you anytime. Let me know when you are.

Warmly,

Fabienne

~~~~~~

Get your free checklist "151 Ways to Attract All The Clients You Need" by sending an e-mail to: ClientAttraction-On@lists.webvalence.com.

Sign up for free teleseminars here: *http://www.clientattraction.com/events_classes.shtml*

If you need more clients, you'll want to visit: *http://www.ClientAttraction.com* for free articles, compelling client testimonials and info on private coaching.

Fabienne Fredrickson, The Client Attraction Expert, Creator of "The Client Attraction System™"

203-595-0068; 866-RAINMAKER (toll free) Fabienne@ClientAttraction.com

~~~~~~

- **Readability:** No matter what the length, your proposal must be delivered in an easy-to-digest format. This means:

  ◪ Clear outline and headings. Place your proposal information in a logical order with distinct section headings. If your proposal is more than a few pages, include a table of contents at the beginning.

  ◪ Bullet points. Bullet points are the best way to present a long list of services or deliverables. Feeling creative? Use clever icons related to your business in place of the standard dots. Caterers might use apples, florists might use sunflowers, financial advisors might use dollar signs.

  ◪ Illustrations. A picture is worth a thousand words, which can translate to thousands of dollars if that picture helps sell the ideas in your proposal. Pie charts, graphs, diagrams, and photographs of products can be the most effective way to explain what you plan to do for a client.

  ◪ Emphasis. When you need to make a topic or idea very clear, put it in **bold**, CAPITAL LETTERS, or underlined text. Make sure your prospect does not miss essential information under any circumstances.

The Content

- **Benchmarks:** You need to know what issues, large and small, are most important to your prospect. Do they care most about low fees? Quick turnaround? Superior quality? If you are not 100 percent clear about key benchmarks, it is okay to ask for specifics. If you can get your prospect to articulate exact success factors, then you'll be able to reflect these back in your proposal—and you can meet, and hopefully exceed, their expectations.

- **Non-starters:** Just as important as what to include is what to *exclude*. Good listening skills include listening for what your prospect does not say. They may not be interested in a large portion of your services that you think are fantastic, so you need to let go of what *you* think your client needs and deliver on what they ask for. Not to worry—if you provide excellent service, you will have an opportunity to expand your services in the future.

■ **Language:** Speak the same language as your prospect. Refer to specific comments that were made at the meeting, or just incorporate some of the terms, phrases, or acronyms you heard the meeting attendees use. It's perfectly acceptable to use some industry jargon in a proposal—show that you are an insider!

■ **News:** You should also demonstrate that you are keeping up on all news about your prospect's industry or company. Include reference to any important information, such as a new product launch or an executive in the news, in your proposal cover letter or in the formal proposal itself.

■ **Additional information:** Now is another good time to speak with anyone you know who has information about your prospect. Compare notes from your pitch meeting with their experiences with your prospect. For instance, if you found your prospect to be less than forthcoming with specifics, ask a mutual friend or colleague if that is the prospect's general nature or if you were not asking the right questions.

■ **Numbers:** Think very carefully about how you use specific numbers—related to price, deliverables, or timing—in your follow-up proposal. Hopefully you have a clear idea of your prospect's expectations from your meeting, so do not stray far from what has already been discussed. I strongly discourage you from broaching the subject of price for the first time in a follow-up proposal. Before including "new" numbers, call your prospect to have the discussion by phone or in person so you know everyone is on the same page—or at least in the same book.

I often recommend that my proposal-writing clients use phrases such as "proposed" or "to be mutually agreed upon" to leave some room for negotiation in their numbers. I also advise showing your proposal to your lawyer and accountant for guidance. Remember that proposals can often be the basis for written contracts, so be cautious about any promises you make in a follow-up proposal.

■ **Letter of Agreement:** If you are ready to close the deal with your follow-up proposal, you may want to consider including a letter of agreement that is separate from the proposal itself. You can use the letter of agreement, which will most likely appear as an attachment at the end of your proposal, as a document to outline the specific deal points that are elaborated upon in the proposal. Again, consult with your lawyer to create this letter.

Above all, as you prepare you proposal, keep in mind that you are developing a relationship that you would like to last for a very long time. Your tone should be positive, collaborative, and forward-thinking.

The Look and Feel

Once you have nailed down your follow-up proposal content, spend time focusing on the look and feel of the proposal. As with the marketing materials you used before and during your pitch, your post-pitch collateral must be perfect. Don't blow it now! Here are some suggestions for packaging and delivery:

- **Be consistently consistent:** Your follow-up proposal needs to continue the look, feel, and tone of your earlier materials. Consistency is a key sign of professionalism, and helps build ongoing credibility and recognition with your prospect. At this point, your prospect should begin to recognize your materials when they cross his or her desk. Why is this so important? When your folder, envelope, and letterhead look familiar, they will shoot to the top of the inbox.

- **Keep personalizing:** Just as you personalized your pitch, make it very clear that you prepared this proposal specifically for your client. Include the company's logo, name, and other specific indicators as often as possible.

- **Be careful:** I am always surprised at how many businesspeople get lazy when they are so close to finalizing a deal. As you did with your pitch presentation, show your follow-up proposal to several trusted friends, family, or colleagues and check for typos, inconsistencies, and errors.

The Contract

The length, terms, and legalese of your contract will vary greatly, depending on the size and scope of the relationship you are about to enter into. I recommend consulting a lawyer, no matter how small your agreement might be, just to make sure you are protected.

For smaller business owners, it can save you time and money to draw up a letter of agreement or contract on your own, then bring it to a lawyer for perfecting. Larry Brower, President of Saratoga Resource Group, LLC, in Charlottesville, Virginia, shares his standard contract, which serves as an excellent accompaniment to a written proposal.

Saratoga
Resource Group LLC
Winning Performance
Through Human Capital

Consulting Agreement

Please see the attached proposal dated December 29, 2005.

Statement of purpose of contract. The XXXX, Inc., of Charlottesville, VA ("XXXX"), wishes to retain the services of the Saratoga Resource Group, LLC, of Charlottesville, VA ("SRG"), for the design and delivery of consulting services related to (1) continued executive coaching through the first quarter of calendar 2006, and (2) facilitation of a set of employee meetings on the HR review project as described in the attached proposal.

Objective of the project. Providing executive coaching services in order to enhance effectiveness, and facilitating meetings designed to deliver employee briefings on the results of the recently completed HR review project.

The services to be delivered. See proposal.

Costs. XXXX agrees to reimburse SRG for services at the rates shown in the proposal. SRG will invoice XXXX monthly for actual time, materials, and expense costs incurred, with a brief description of each item. XXXX agrees that such invoices will be paid within 30 days; otherwise a finance charge of 1.5% per month will apply on the outstanding balance.

Expenses. With adequate substantiation, XXXX will reimburse SRG for all reasonable travel, lodging, and meal expenses incurred by SRG staff in connection with any travel requested by XXXX.

XXXX role in the project. For any meetings, XXXX will schedule and arrange the attending participants, program site, supporting services such as food and beverage, audio/visual equipment, paper and pencils, name tags and name tents, and any other materials or equipment related to participants or the site.

SRG role in the project. SRG will provide facilitators, assessment materials, PowerPoint presentations or overhead slides, laptop computer, and any other materials or equipment related to the project and its components to be carried out by SRG.

Confidentiality. SRG and all SRG staff agree that this agreement creates a confidential relationship between XXXX and SRG, and that information concerning XXXX's employees, business affairs, plans, customers, vendors, finances, properties, methods of operation, and other such information, is confidential in nature. Confidential information shall not be released by either party without the express written consent of the owner of the confidential information.

Material copyrights. Material will be copyrighted to both SRG and XXXX, with each page and each slide carrying the legend "© Saratoga Resource Group. Use outside XXXX prohibited."

Staffing. Larry Brower, President of SRG, will be the lead consultant on the project. It is understood that all SRG staff are independent contractors, and not employees or agents of XXXX. SRG consultants will be responsible for all relevant taxes as independent contractors. SRG staff shall have no authority to bind XXXX or incur other obligations on behalf of XXXX.

In the event that SRG provides additional consulting staff other than Brower, XXXX will have right of review of the additional consultants' background, experience, and credentials before the consultants are hired by SRG for the project.

Termination of contract. This agreement may be terminated at any time, and for any reason, by either XXXX or SRG. In such case, any fees or reimbursable expenses due SRG would be payable as described above.

Proposal. The attached proposal is incorporated into this Consulting Agreement and together constitute the entire Agreement between the parties.

XXXX, Inc.

By: ___[*Client's name*]___   By: ___[*Your name*]___

Name printed:_____   Name printed: _____

Title:_____   Title: _____

Date:_____   Date: _____

The Delivery

I strongly believe that proposals are best delivered in person. Schedule a time to meet with your prospect to present your ideas and work through additional details face-to-face. This will help you come to an agreement as quickly and efficiently as possible and will help you avoid any misunderstandings. Avoid a situation where you are submitting multiple follow-up proposals with small changes in each one.

If you cannot meet in person, set up a conference call to go over the proposal, make any requested changes, and then send the proposal to your prospect by overnight mail. Now is the time to get your prospect to agree to all of the great things you discussed in your pitch meeting. If you have carefully developed your relationship and followed all of the guidelines for a successful, targeted pitch, then closing the deal should be the easy part!

Not satisfied with a simple overnight mail package? Once you have met with a prospect and established a relationship, you might want to consider a more creative way of delivering your proposal. If you are pitching UPS, use UPS. The key is to be creative in a way that relates to your product or service—there needs to be a logical and clever connection. Don't send your proposal in a pizza box if you are a photographer!

Give Them Something They Haven't Paid for Yet

I believe there is a crucial component to the follow-up proposal that has absolutely nothing to do with the proposal document itself. It is something I have been doing for years and I believe it has "put me over the top" on several deals. Here is what I do: Sometime between a pitch meeting and the finalizing of a new business proposal, I always give my prospect a pre-deal "bonus" of consulting advice or privileged information. For example, because one of my specialties is marketing to small businesses, I might send a potential corporate client an article I have written about the buying habits of small business owners.

Many people are afraid to "give away" their services before signing a contract, but this is not what I am advocating. My advice is to be a consultant—to act as a trusted advisor and resource. This adds to your credibility and demonstrates your desire to be a true partner to your prospect. As a bonus, I believe that there are only so many times someone will accept free advice before feeling a desire to pay for your valuable counsel.

On this note, if you feel that you are offering advice, consultation, or information that has a very high value, it is appropriate to indicate this to your prospect by sending an invoice with the service described and priced, and the amount due marked as "Complimentary." This is very common practice for interior decorators, financial advisors, agents, or other professionals who provide a free consultation before a client signs on formally. Do not be afraid to follow this model for your business.

This strategy works well for product-based businesses as well. Such famous brands as Smartfood and Mrs. Fields began with their founders giving away products to create buzz. While this has become relatively common practice for many product entrepreneurs (especially when the product is edible), you can stand out from the crowd by offering a prospect a taste (pun intended!) of a new product that may be in development and not available to anyone else yet. Everyone loves an inside scoop.

Be a Buzz Builder

Why is it so important to provide some freebie products or services to your prospects? It's marketing! Even during advanced stages of the pitch process when you are on the verge of a deal, you still need to continue marketing yourself and your products. In fact, as you will learn in later chapters, you will continue to market throughout your entire relationship with any client.

Sampling helps to create buzz for your product or service, and buzz-building, or "word-of-mouth" marketing, is an extremely effective strategy. In fact, *Fast Company* magazine featured a Boston-based business that helps companies build buzz for their new products. BzzAgent, LLC, has created a database of "agents" that clients can access to test their product and build word of mouth in their communities for a new product. Agents work for free in order to be "in the know" and to receive and use products and services targeted to their particular demographic. This is an important point: People who are suited to your product or service are happy to promote it for free, if they like it. Of course, they will also bad mouth it if they don't like it!

How can you be a buzz-builder for your business? Begin by offering a complimentary service or product to prospects you are pitching. If this proves to be an effective strategy, you can begin to expand your buzz-building to new prospects. You will not only be helping to close deals, but also to build word of mouth that will spread to new prospects in the future (see Chapter 9).

Section

III

After: Creating

Lifelong Customers

Chapter 7

Don't Peak Too Early: The Art of Gentle Persistence

No matter what "next steps" were determined at the end of your pitch meeting and laid out in your written proposal, it's your job to close the deal and get your relationship rolling. Now that you have produced and delivered your follow-up proposal, it's time to create a focused, follow-up action plan. Carolyn Sawyer, owner of the Tom Sawyer Company, a marketing, advertising, and public relations company in Columbia, South Carolina, says she has found that "the three most important things to do after a pitch are follow up, follow up, and follow up." I could not agree more. However, the trick is to be persistent without being, well, obnoxious.

You must continue to be strategic and manage the final stage of the pitch process. To invoke some tempting baseball terminology, you must make the switch from starting pitcher to closer. This chapter offers a variety of different follow-up tactics. Read through and pick and choose the strategies that are right for your particular situation.

Establish Your Desired Reach and Frequency of Contact

Your "persistence plan" will depend on several factors. Consider the following dynamics to determine not only how persistent you need to be, but also what method of follow-up will be most effective and efficient to get you to a "yes."

- **Your prospect company's structure:** How many people are involved in the decision-making process? If you have pitched a consumer, sole proprietor, or small business owner, you are likely dealing with the decision-making faculties of only one person. If you have pitched a division of a large corporation or government organization, your proposal may need to be approved by several individuals. Either way, always correspond with your main contact. It is never a good idea to go over the head of your main contact, or to follow up with several people at once. This is a quick way to alienate your potential clients and sour them on a relationship with you. It is also a waste of your time; colleagues compare notes, so there is no need or advantage to calling everyone you know at your prospect company.

- **Your prospect's personal style:** Over the course of the pitch process you have no doubt become an expert on your prospect; now is the time to use all of the information you have gathered. Personality types can differ greatly, so take some time to think about the personal and professional style of the prospect you have pitched— enthusiastic, reserved, cautious, procrastinating, and so on—when waiting for a response.

- **Your competition:** You may have a bit of a wait if your pitch was in response to a Request for Proposals (RFP). Your prospect may be meeting with several competing companies all vying for their business. These meetings can take several weeks to several months, so if this is the case with your pitch, be careful not to pester—there are clearly many others ready and willing to win the same business.

- **The economy:** Stock market dips, industry indicators, and other economic factors from the greater business world have an enormous effect on some industries. Depending on your prospect and your industry, be aware of the local, regional, national, and even international economy.

- **The calendar:** Did you pitch just before the December holidays? In the middle of the hottest week of summer? Just before school vacation (and, therefore, family vacation) week in April? The day before a blizzard? Every season of the year is full of holidays, events, and weather patterns that can lead to short- or long-term delays in the business world. Mother Nature and Father Time may or may not be on your side.

Smart, Simple Tactics

Here are some successful follow-up strategies offered by business-people in a variety of industries and geographic locations:

Follow up often, gently, and sincerely.

—Montana Gray,
Delray Beach, Florida

Follow up with the potential client to add one more suggestion or referral that was not discussed at the meeting or in your written proposal.

—Charles Donovan, Wellness Publishers, LLC,
St. Louis, Missouri

Send a hand-written, informal note showing that you have listened to what your prospect's needs are.

—Sandy Smith, SLS Creative Business Solutions,
Cypress, California

Send an e-mail or note with an easy marketing tip [that was not mentioned previously] that the prospect could implement immediately.

—Anonymous small business owner

Send a one-page recap of action items and delivery dates.

—George F. Gaines, Nexagen USA,
Orlando, Florida

Offer to help the prospect find someone else for another one of their business needs, free of charge. [In other words, be a matchmaker and show off your good connections!]

—Kelly Brereton, SagePath,
Atlanta, Georgia

Mistakes to Avoid

It is just as important to avoid mistakes in your follow-up as it is to take the right steps. Some lessons learned might save you the pain of experiencing them for yourself. For example, don't mention your competition in a pitch meeting! I once witnessed a client rave about Katie Couric and the *Today* show—produced by NBC—to executives at CBS! (I'll keep the client anonymous, for obvious reasons!) And, as Diane Hill Craver of Cary, North Carolina, points out, "Don't forget to ask for the sale or to suggest the next step." It sounds simple, but it's amazing how many people never actually make "the ask," even in a written proposal.

Continue to Serve as a Trusted and Valued Resource

If your waiting period is prolonged due to the factors listed above or the myriad other reasons why the world never moves as quickly as we desire, don't just sit with your hands folded. Beyond leaving the requisite voice-mail and e-mail messages (explored in more detail in the next section), reach out to your prospect in memorable and creative ways:

- **Send articles of interest.** Scour daily newspapers, industry publications, online newsletters, and magazines for articles that would interest your prospect. Forward them in e-mail or hard copy format with a brief note, "Thought this might interest you." Don't mention your proposal. Forwarded articles can relate to personal (such as a sports team or hobby your prospect mentioned) or professional issues. Whatever you do, don't forward joke e-mails, chain letters, or anything off-color or controversial. You want to stay on your prospect's radar screen and demonstrate your value as an ongoing resource.

- **Recognize their accomplishments.** As you are noting articles of interest, also be on the lookout for any news about your prospect's company. Recognize any new products, events, promotions, or news with a brief note of congratulations.

- **Inform your prospect of your accomplishments.** Share any good news about your business as soon as possible: new products, new clients, good press, or new employee hires. If you are uncomfortable tooting your own horn, then consider including your prospect on a general distribution list for a press release or newsletter from your company announcing your newest achievements.

- **Invite your prospect to events.** Particularly during a long waiting period, try to find ways to invite your prospect to get together in person in a non-meeting setting—*as your guest*. If you are connected in your community, you should be receiving regular invitations to such events as charity functions, receptions, conferences, art exhibits, sporting events, lectures, and trade shows. If you are not as connected as you might like, then look to the calendars in your local newspaper or chamber of commerce Website for appropriate events at which you can invite a prospect to join you. Be on the lookout for events that would benefit your prospect's business—then you have a much better chance of acceptance.

  If you forward an invitation and your prospect accepts, great. RSVP on behalf of your prospect (and double check that his or her name is on the guest list and spelled correctly so a name badge will be waiting) and pay in advance for both of your admission fees. Just like paying for a pitch meeting lunch, consider this the cost of doing business (and a small price to pay for more time alone with your prospect).

  If you forward an invitation and your prospect declines, that is okay too. You have shown yourself to be a connected, active person with a generous attitude and a desire to deepen your relationship with your prospect. That's better than a "Just writing to follow up on the proposal I sent" e-mail message any day.

- **Show up where your prospect might be.** Attend industry events, association meetings, chamber of commerce functions, or any event where you think your prospect or his or her colleagues may be. Don't be a stalker, but do say hello and make conversation. The extra face-time may spark your prospect to move your proposal to the top of the pile.

- **Connect through mutual contacts.** When possible, try to connect with your prospect through mutual acquaintances or professional affiliations. Attend events where the prospect's colleagues are likely to be, or phone or e-mail a shared colleague to say hello and update them on your potential deal with the prospect. This will keep you close to your prospect because, even if you do not actually make contact through these methods, you can still be visible through a casual mention by a colleague or a picture of you in a professional association event report.

- **Show that you have a good memory.** Recall specific details from your meeting or specific facts about your prospect and acknowledge them when possible. For instance, if a person's birthday occurs during a waiting period, send a card. If the company is launching a new campaign, send a good luck card. If your prospect's son is graduating from college, send a congratulations e-card.

Be Pleasantly Persistent Without Being Obnoxious

If your pitch meeting went well and your prospect responded positively to your written proposal, it is likely that only a few calls or e-mails will be necessary to seal the deal. However, sometimes you will not get a response after your first follow-up communication. Or your second. Or your third....

Yes, sometimes business can be like dating: You have a great first date, then a great second date, and then the person never calls again. So what do you do if you feel like you are being stood up? If you have attempted to contact your prospect and have not received a response in a week or more, or during the time frame you and your prospect agreed to in person, follow this simple action plan:

1. Do not panic! The quickest way to screw up a business relationship is to jump to conclusions and do something rash like driving angrily to your prospect's place of business and demanding an explanation for a lack of returned phone calls. Life happens—kids get sick, business emergencies occur, employees quit, etc., etc.—and the lack of response from your prospect may have absolutely nothing to do with

you or your pitch. If you want to stealthily check on your prospect's whereabouts, anonymously contact a receptionist, assistant, or other lower level employee, simply to ask if your main contact has been in the office.

Cookie Wherry, creator of the WEDGIE—"The world's best gardening tool"—shares a story of persistence that perfectly demonstrates the "don't panic" principle:

> "I spoke to the buyer at Lewis Ginter Botanical Garden on the phone June 4, asking her to look at my Website, *www.wedgie.biz*. She e-mailed on June 5 with questions. She seemed really interested. I e-mailed back all the answers the next day.
>
> "Then I heard nothing. I could have assumed that my answers made her change her mind and she was no longer interested. But I didn't. I sent an e-mail on the 15th saying I remembered that she'd said space was tight in the gift shop until September because they were redoing the outdoor garden area of the shop, so if the two dozen minimum was a problem, the order could be less. She immediately e-mailed back that she'd been out of the office for a week, would be back by the end of the week, and would call in an order.
>
> "Had I not persisted, WEDGIE would probably have dropped from her mind and I'd never have heard from her!"

I would add that Cookie wisely showed her flexibility and offered new information in her follow-up e-mail, explaining that her minimum order requirements could be relaxed. It is also my secret belief that people can't resist opening an e-mail with the word "WEDGIE" in the subject line!

2. Attempt to make one contact each by phone, cell phone, and e-mail. Do not rule out the possibility of technology snafus. I once experienced a computer meltdown that resulted in three days' worth of lost e-mails, and we have all had the experience of accidentally deleting a voice-mail message from our cell phones. Try all available contact methods, just in case the one you are trying is not working.

Persistence@Persistence.com

PR expert Ginny Shea of Mixed Media Publicity & Promotion shares an e-mail she sent to an unresponsive prospect to whom she was pitching a jazz trio. I particularly like Ginny's casual tone (perfect for the music industry) and the way she directly states her client's commitment to serving the needs of this prospect. According to Ginny, this e-mail message prompted a response and won her client a spot in a popular music festival.

Subject: room for WBJ?

Hi,

Spoke to Johnny again today about squeezing World's Best Jazz into the conference festivities of Biggest Music Fest. I know you're very busy handling major acts, but I would love to get in contact with you soon to see what we can do for our jazz trio, World's Best Jazz. The trio is just coming off a successful CD release party for their new CD, and has recently had many opportunities offered to them in the Northwest area in the month of September. By far, this conference is their top priority while on the West Coast, but we need an idea as to the reality of their booking opportunity so we can confirm other dates/venues as well. Thank you for your time and hope to hear from you soon.

Best,

G

3. Likewise, check that all of your phones and e-mail addresses are working properly. Double check any "junk mail" or "bulk mail" folders to make sure a vital message did not accidentally end up there.

4. In the event that your first set of messages is not received, wait one week (or an amount of time you feel is appropriate, based on your knowledge of your prospect), then you may follow up again by phone or e-mail. If you do leave a new message, do not simply repeat your first message. Instead, mention that you are calling again and provide new information, such as an update on the status of your company or a suggestion of a resource that you have not mentioned before. Remain positive and energetic in your tone— never betray your frustration at not receiving a return call.

5. If you do not receive a return call or e-mail after several attempts, you may have misread your prospect's intention to work with you. As a last resort, follow up with a written correspondence, reiterating the main points in your proposal and include a self-addressed stamped envelope with a response card stating the prospect's interest in working with you.

   If you do receive a "no" response, even after all of the hard work you have put into your pitch, do not take it to heart. It's business, not personal. Really.

6. Sometimes price is the sticking point. If you suspect (or know) that your prospect is hesitating because of the price of your products or services, consider a special offer. You don't want to create a losing financial situation for your company, but it can help to think about creative ways to lower your prices, perhaps on a certain product, or for a limited time. Larry Bower of the Saratoga Resource Group, LLC, in Charlottesville, Virginia, sends out special pricing announcements to nudge his prospects to sign on the dotted line.

Creative Follow-Up Tactics

Feeling gutsy? Here are some fun examples of creative persistence. Think outside the box and you may see results faster than you imagined!

Pot Luck

I once had a travel agency as a client, and it was pitching its corporate travel services to a variety of companies. The agency had a difficult time hearing back from these companies after its pitch meeting, so the agency decided to send out a box that said on the top, "We know your decision to choose a travel agency has been put on the back burner...." Inside the box there was another sheet of paper that said, "We hope this helps move it to the front." Enclosed was a potholder with their company logo on it. The travel agency ended up closing several deals because its prospects found this idea innovative, creative, and fun.

One to Grow On

Stephanie Cohen and Hayley Byer, of Verge Promotional Marketing, move their deals closer to closing by sending a cute flower pot containing soil and seeds. The attached note reads, "We want to grow your business."

Virtual Tactics

In a more "New Economy" tactic, the owners of Verge demonstrate their technical savvy by sending an animated graphic to prospects they have recently pitched. Following a pitch to a large insurance company, Verge e-mailed a Macromedia Flash animation movie to all seven attendees of the pitch meeting. The movie featured the Verge logo and the insurance company's logo flying into an envelope. When the logos arrived safely inside, the envelope closed and a message appeared on the screen: "Let's seal the deal." According to Stephanie, the company's chief marketing officer called immediately to hire the creative team.

Summer Fun

For my company, Impression Impact, I was sending information to CEOs targeting the small business market and wanted to do something extra to attract their interest. The mailing coincided with the beginning of the summer season, so I contacted an ad specialty company and had them design a mesh beach bag and flip flops with my company name imprinted. Along with the bag and sandals I printed a card that said, "Summer Reading Material Enclosed." It sure beat trying to get CEOs on the phone in the lazy, hazy days of June and July!

Relaxation Nation

Carolyn Sawyer of the Tom Sawyer Company in Columbia, South Carolina, follows up with a thoughtful gift, such as a neck pillow for prospects who travel often. She accompanies the neck pillows with a handwritten note that says, "Relax and leave it to us."

When Persistence Pays Off

Hopefully your persistence will lead to the word you've been waiting seven chapters to hear: "yes." All of your hard work will pay off in the deal itself and in the discipline you have developed along the path of pitching. Many of the activities you have performed to this point, from research to networking to building relationships to persistence and perseverance, will be necessary components of servicing your new client, winning increasing business from them, and securing new clients in the future.

But before you turn the page and graduate from a pitcher to a winner, take a moment to pat yourself on the back. Congratulations!

Chapter 8

The Art of Overdelivery

I know what you are thinking: "The pitch is over and I won the new business. Why is the book still going?" The final and most important part of pitching new business is delivering—no, overdelivering—on the promises you made throughout the pitch process and continuing to market your business even when you have a full client load.

Even when an initial business deal is signed and sealed, you need to maintain the activities you have developed to this point. By following the advice in the final three chapters of this book, you'll find you'll have to make fewer pitches, because you'll be winning more and more business and referrals from your existing clients. The art of overdelivery involves fulfilling the promises made in your pitch and post-pitch negotiations, plus offering new and unexpected forms of service, support, and surprise. No matter what your field—from sales, to financial services, to law, to catering, to writing, to consulting—you are now in the business of customer service.

Start With a Bang...and a Breaking of Bread

A new business relationship is like a new personal relationship. You begin by getting to know each other. This is the time to be polite, accommodating, impressive, and more than willing to compromise. It may take a while for you and your new client to become comfortable in a business relationship with one another, so be sensitive to your client's pace. Different clients become trusting and loyal over differing lengths of time, and it often happens one day or one project at a time. You have already cultivated your prospect into a client. Next, your challenge is to advance your client into an advocate who will help you win new business in the future. Chapter 9 will address this topic in detail.

To get started on the right foot, let your client know from day one how important he or she is. While I began the book with the premise that you have been pitching your biggest dream prospect, you must treat all new clients—even your smallest—like gold. You never know which clients may start small and end up growing bigger and bigger.

I like to begin every new client relationship with a celebratory lunch. This is especially important if you have not previously taken a meal with your client. I bring this up primarily because of my own experience in having met Bruce Nelson for lunch and then winning Office Depot as a client. However, something I have not yet mentioned is that, after bidding $1,050 to meet and have lunch with Mr. Nelson, the following year I spent $1,300 dollars at the same charity auction to have lunch with him again! I wanted to thank him for introducing me to key executives at his company who gave me a contract. The second lunch further solidified our connection. While most *Fortune* 500 CEOs probably have business lunches every day, many businesspeople rarely receive an invitation to leave the office for a nice lunch. Particularly if your new client owns a small or medium-sized business, he or she may seldom enjoy a nice free meal.

Besides thanking your new client by providing them with the gift of lunch, you are also creating an opportunity for your client to learn more about you and your business. This can speed the process of building mutual trust and loyalty. Meeting for a meal is also a nice opportunity to invite other key members of your team and/or the client's team who may be working closely together on the day-to-day details. There is just something about sharing a meal—the classic "breaking of bread"—that makes for a deeper level of connection. We like to do business with people we know and trust, and the sharing and enjoying of a meal adds to our knowledge of each other.

Announce It to the World

Winning new business is reason to celebrate with the client, but also with the world. Share your good news! Here are some suggestions for making the most of the positive momentum of a new client:

■ Contact the person responsible for your new client's public relations to coordinate efforts. This may be the client himself or herself (if it is a sole proprietorship), an outside agency, or an entire communications department. Ask your client with whom to speak and coordinate efforts. Note that in a few instances, such as law or the security industry, your client will request that your new relationship remain confidential. However, in most cases, your client will be eager to share in any publicity you generate about your new partnership. Be sure to share any press releases, articles, or other publicly released announcements with your new client to ensure accuracy of message, spelling, and other key details.

■ Add your new client's name and logo to your Website and promotional kit. I like to feature new clients on the homepage of my Website, to show them their importance to my business and to announce to other site visitors that my company is successfully winning new business. Most companies will also appreciate it if you add a link on your Website from the client's company name or logo to their Website.

■ Write and send a press release. I recommend e-mailing the press release (possibly as a component of an existing online newsletter, if you have one) to your entire database, including current clients, prospects, vendors, partners, friends, family, and the media. Speaking of the media, I can't emphasis enough how much I wish I had pursued more media coverage in the early years of my business. Don't be shy or afraid to let the media know about your business. If you can, try to relate your new client to current events and piggyback off of existing news. For instance, if you run a business in the fitness industry and you have won a new client, tie the announcement to current statistics on Americans and obesity. Or if you are a small business consultant, relate your story to current economic indicators in your city or region.

- Send your press release, or simply an announcement blurb, to publications that have a "member announcements" or "members on the move" type of section. These sections are designed for new client announcements or business deals, so take full advantage! You never know who may see your name or your company featured in a publication and then contact you because of it. Let the new business queries come to you!

- If a publication does feature an article or blurb about your new client relationship, maximize the exposure you receive. Your business may not skyrocket the second you end up with an article about your company, however, you can reprint it, produce really nice color copies, and include them in your presentation kit and format a PDF to add to your Website. Any media article is like a highly credible marketing piece that you didn't have to pay for!

Educate Your Staff and Business Partners

If you run a business with one or 1,000 employees, you need to make sure that everyone in your company is informed about your new client relationship. As I have said over and over again, people want to do business with people they know, so make sure your employees are part of the equation. Remember an important rule of customer service: Serve your employees first so that they can serve your customer.

Just as you put out a press release to announce your new client relationship to the public, you need to announce the relationship to your employees in a formal, detailed way. While large companies may enjoy the benefit of an internal corporate communications department, smaller companies can follow a similar protocol. You need to educate your employees about their role in the projects to come. This is also an opportunity to share success with your employees. Make them feel part of the excitement that you are no doubt feeling.

Host an internal company lunch or pizza party, to share the details of the new client relationship. This shares your success with everyone in your company and encourages buy-in and loyalty. You will want to provide employees at all levels of your company with the following general information:

◪ Names, titles, and reporting structure of the key employees with whom you will be working. Make sure everyone recognizes these names and understands the function of each person in case they receive a phone call or e-mail from the new client.

◪ An overview of the core business of the new client, particularly if it is a product or service your company has not encountered previously.

◪ An overview of the products or services you will be providing to this client. What area of your business will be affected?

◪ Crucial company changes caused by the new client relationship. Change is always a little bit scary, so address any questions or concerns your employees may have. For instance, will you be hiring new staff? Will you be working with new vendors? Will you or any of your staff members be required to travel more frequently? If you do not know the answers to these or other important questions at this point, make note of any employee queries and make a commitment to answer them as soon as you are able.

If you work with outside vendors—which is often the case with sole proprietors, independent salespeople, or small business owners—inform your vendors and partners of your new client as well. Your new client relationship may represent increased work for them, so they are sure to be interested and responsive. This is particularly important if your business partners will have any direct contact with your new client. Your client will likely see partners as an extension of your customer service, so make sure they are representing you in the strongest possible way.

I cannot emphasize enough how important it is to cultivate buy-in from all parties when a new business relationship is established. I have a young employee in my office and I say to him almost daily, "The objective here is to make it very easy for our clients. That's really what we're supposed to be doing. We don't want to go back to them and make it difficult for them to do something. We just want to make it easy for them to do business with us, because they'll want to continue to do that." Remember your mantra: "Customer service, customer service, customer service."

Educate Your Client and Develop Internal Advocates

Just as you need to educate and ensure buy-in from your employees, it is also your job to do whatever you can to help educate and win over the staff of your new client's company. While you certainly have less control over these people, you can offer to help in any way you can: by providing materials about your business to your new client, creating a "Clients Only" area of your Website to provide them with ongoing information, and adding your client's employees (with their permission, of course) to any regular correspondence you send about your business and this client relationship, in particular.

It is important at this point to reemphasize the politics of client relationships. Do not, under any circumstances, go "over the head" of your primary client contact. Clear any and all plans for correspondence with your primary contact and keep this person in the loop at all times. Communication is one of the key elements of good customer service. Keep everyone in the loop and you will avoid many potential problems.

Hit Your Deadlines

No matter how big or complicated your first assignment for a new client, you must hit your first deadline. This may go without saying, but there is no worse way to start a new relationship than to under-deliver on your first assignment. In fact, try to complete your first assignment *before* your deadline and you are sure to impress. I am always pleasantly surprised—and extremely impressed—when I check my e-mail or mailbox and find a project delivered before a deadline I have set with a vendor.

Develop Regular Reporting Methods

In order for a company to understand what you are doing for them and the value you are providing, you need to tell them. And tell them often.

Here is a sample of the regular reports I provide to Office Depot on the Web Café series I coordinate:

impression impact

Web Café Bi-Monthly Report

January/February Series

Steps completed by Impression Impact for January/February Web Café series:

- Identified and confirmed the line-up for 2004 kick off of Web Café Series
- Coached presenters on the title of their programs and PowerPoint considerations
- Wrote web copy for line-up
- Promoted the Web Café in Nancy Michael's e-zine Michaels on Marketing (5000+ opt-in subscribers)
- Worked with Jay Abraham and Jerry Weissman on the description of their presentation (had some challenging conversations regarding some minor adjustments to their program and explained how to "push" the slides forward for better individual control over the presentation)
- Edited and refined their existing PowerPoint presentations to conform to the Office Depot template
- Communicated with their assistants until the days prior to the Web Café when Nancy Michaels coached the speaker and his assistant on the process of participating in the Web Café, etc.
- Wrote introductions for the entire series

- Completed Top 10 Lists/highlights of Web Café's content to be distributed to participants
- Supplying the transcripts of each web cast as a courtesy to the speaker
- Nancy will host two of the upcoming Web Cafés

Feedback received:

- 3000 Registered participants on the Web Café for Jay Abraham (600 actually on the line) John is looking into why this occurred
- 300 Registered participants for Jerry Weissman
- Followed-up with FairyTale Brownies to each speaker and his assistant with personal phone call thanking them for the presentation, etc.

Next Steps (see attached):

- Please review next line-up of proposed guests. I'd like your feedback on them, so I can begin to finalize the next round of speakers.
- Working on a one-sheet to explain how to maximize and leverage the speaker's marketing potential among their own prospects and customers

Request Feedback

When I first began my business, I was a bit shy about requesting feedback—both positive and negative—from my clients. Perhaps I was fearful. Now I request feedback every chance I get. I find it the most effective way to continually serve my clients with the kind of service they most desire. I don't think it is ever too early to begin an open dialogue with clients about their satisfaction with your work. Not only will you receive valuable feedback from the get-go, but your clients will also feel valued and listened to. Here are some tips for requesting and analyzing client feedback in the most effective way:

■ **Commit to understanding your client's definition of value—today, tomorrow, and forever.** Knowing what is most important to your client and then delivering on it is your most important job. Because this definition of value is likely to change over time (and perhaps frequently, with a difficult client!) due to the ebbs and flows of the business world, you need to constantly reassess your value proposition. Your first articulation of value was in your post-pitch meeting proposal, so use that document as your starting point.

■ **Establish a method of formal client research.** Depending on the size of your business, you should invest in a trustworthy method of researching your client needs. In the next section I go into specific detail about surveying, which I find to be the most effective method for soliciting both positive and negative feedback.

■ **Continue to solicit informal client feedback.** Even when you have implemented a formal means for assessing client satisfaction, you can and should solicit feedback informally, as well. For instance, we can all hear it in someone's voice when they are unhappy. Rather than ignoring someone's unpleasant or stressed tone of voice, *ask* if anything is wrong and if there is anything you can do to improve your client's situation, whether their dissatisfaction has something to do with you or not. Remember, your goal is not only to provide excellent service to your client for the work you have been hired to perform, but also to serve as a trusted guide and resource *in general*. Never miss an opportunity to provide service. And if the problem *is* related to your work, you want to know sooner rather than later, so you can make the appropriate changes to improve your client's satisfaction immediately. Never let a grudge build. As Jill Griffin, of The Griffin Group, wisely advised in her May 11, 2004 article "12 Laws of Customer Loyalty" for the Website MarketingProfs.com:

> For most companies, only 10% of complaints get articulated by customers. The other 90% are unarticulated and manifest themselves in many negative ways: unpaid invoices, lack of courtesy to your frontline service reps and, above all, negative word of mouth. With the Internet, an unhappy customer can now reach thousands of your would-be customers in a few keystrokes. Head off bad

press before it happens. Make it easy for customers to complain, and treat complaints seriously. Establish firm guidelines regarding customer response time, reporting and trend analysis. Make employee complaint monitoring a key tool for executive decision-making.

Surveying Is Marketing

As you can see, even though people might be thinking many good or bad thoughts about your work, it's actually very rare to receive that feedback without specifically asking for it. It's also helpful to have somebody who is not directly involved in your business to do that. For my business, I have retained the expert Susan LaPlante Dube of Precision Marketing Group (*www.precisionmarketinggroup.com*) to help me survey my clients by telephone. I will share Susan's advice and expertise for this method of surveying, as well as discussing the use of online surveys, which is another helpful and more cost-effective method of soliciting client feedback.

While surveying is a crucial activity to conduct with a new client— and it is certainly a key customer service initiative—Susan LaPlante Dube has taught me that we really need to think about surveying as a key *marketing* initiative. It should be part of everyone's marketing plan done at least on an annual basis, but ideally every six months, if you have a large number of customers to cycle through.

Surveying should be part of the ongoing process, because you do receive some incredible feedback that can help you make adjustments in your business. Of course, you don't want to be adjusting your business to the whim of every comment, but it's going to allow you to see patterns in your customers' experiences, and they are absolutely the best people to give you some feedback on what's working well and what's not.

Whether you are surveying a new client or surveying your entire database, here are nine steps to follow for maximum surveying success:

Step 1: State Your Goal

What is the purpose of surveying your customers or clients? Is it to find out if your customer service is good? Is it to determine their perception of your services or product? Is it to identify pricing trends or industry trends? Is it to test new messaging? There are numerous reasons why you might do this, but you really want to sit down and think about what your goal is, because that's going to drive everything else that occurs in the process.

Step 2: Determine Qualitative vs. Quantitative

Next, based on your goal and on the volume of customers you have, you need to determine if this is going to be a qualitative or a quantitative survey. Qualitative surveys involve free-form, open-ended questions. Chances are, you would use a third party to conduct qualitative phone interviews. For this you need to find somebody objective and outside your business—such as Susan LaPlante Dube—because your customers will be much more open to providing feedback that may be difficult for them to say.

Susan has shared with me the example of an architectural firm she worked with. The client was losing business and couldn't understand why. After they lost a major client—they were designing a $2-million home—they called Susan and asked her to survey their customers. One of the architect's clients revealed that they liked him very, very, very much and didn't want to hurt his feelings. This actually worked against the architect, because whenever the firm asked this client if he was satisfied, the client would say, "I love your design." The architectural firm went on thinking that the client was satisfied, but when Susan called, he said, "I love their design but…," then gave a litany of all the things the architect did wrong. The architectural firm was losing business because customers didn't want to hurt their feelings!

This is why it is critical to have somebody outside the business perform your surveying, particularly if you are currently losing business or suspect that a client is unhappy. Somebody outside the business can also be objective in terms of seeing patterns that may slip your notice, simply because you're too close to your business to look at it objectively.

If you decide on a quantitative survey, you will seek out numerical, quantifiable data. This type of survey helps you to find trends, and it is a great way to gather large volumes of data. If there are some very specific metrics that you want to establish and measure over time, a quantitative survey is the way to go.

However, a qualitative survey is going to give you much deeper information than a quantitative survey. Even if you have 200 or 300 customers, Susan suggests always probing further with seven to 10 clients. Ask them to participate in a qualitative phone survey—one you develop from the information you gathered in the quantitative survey. According to Susan, surveying 10 clients can give you enough feedback to provide insight into all of your customers' satisfaction and attitudes.

Be sure that your third-party surveyor assures your clients that their responses will be kept strictly confidential, if this is the case. They are much more likely to say the whole truth and nothing but the truth. If you want to know which clients provide what feedback, be honest about this fact. Honesty is the only policy when it comes to surveys.

Step 3: Choose Your Method

You have several options regarding how you will conduct your survey. Following are three options to consider: third-party surveyor, online surveying, and mailed surveys.

Third-Party Surveyors

Human surveyors can often elicit information that online or mailed surveys cannot. I find third-party surveyors to be most effective for important customer research. I then supplement this service with online surveys about specific topics.

Susan shared with me the story of one of her clients in the Website optimization field. This particular client did a tremendous amount of work via e-mail with her customers, and she seldom picked up the phone to talk to them. As a result, she felt disconnected to her clients so she opted for live surveying by phone. Susan surveyed seven customers. Afterwards, once she had all the data, the business owner made appointments with all seven customers to tell them about the results and actually ended up closing business with six out of the seven. A quarter later, after the surveying, she had increased her business by 70 percent!

How do you select a partner for the sensitive work of surveying your clients and colleagues? When selecting a third-party surveyor, my best advice is to ask your friends and colleagues for a recommendation.

Remember that this person will be speaking one-on-one with your valued clients, potential clients, past clients, and other business associates, so you want to find someone who will represent you in the most professional way possible. Check referrals, and if you desire, ask to hear audiotapes of the surveyor at work.

Prices can vary widely, but are usually based on an initial set-up and management fee, plus a price per survey conducted.

Online Surveys

The major advantage to online surveying is clearly the cost—or lack of cost. You can create an online survey through such free providers as surveymonkey.com or zoomerang.com and send them to as many people as you wish. While online surveys are somewhat limited in scope, you can generally ask both quantitative and qualitative questions. Many people are wary of the confidentiality of online methods, so be extra careful in your instructions and follow-up. Explain that the survey is coming from you and be clear about whether or not the responses are anonymous.

Another advantage of online surveys is that the software manages responses for you, tallying results into handy charts, graphs, and statistics. I use online surveys often and have found them extremely useful.

Mailed Surveys

Sending a survey through the mail is another option, although it can be quite costly because of printing and postage fees. The advantage to a hard copy document is that people may take more time to provide responses than they would with an online survey. Be sure to provide a prepaid envelope for responses, and follow up aggressively to remind people to mail back the forms.

Step 4: Create Your Questions Carefully

If you are working with an outside person, he or she can help you create questions. You want to be very direct and very specific about what you're asking. If somebody looks at a question and it could be interpreted two or three ways, that's not a good question, because you will never know what kind of feedback you're getting, particularly on a quantitative survey.

Be very direct, be very specific. Ask questions such as:

◪ "What specific value have you received?"

◪ "Can you quantify the value of working with us?"

◪ "Would you provide a testimonial?"

◪ "What are strengths of this organization and its service or product?"

◪ "What are areas for improvement?"

◪ "What additional services could we provide for you?"

Be sure you're asking for *exactly* what you want. Susan provides a great example of a client who did sound and video installation. When she was talking to one of their corporate customers, she asked the question, "How can we reach more decision-makers like you?" The person replied, "Well, the first thing you could do is just ask me. I can think of three companies I would refer them to." The company had just never picked up the phone to make that call! Had they not asked that question in a survey, they would have never had found three additional prospective customers recommended by the company surveyed. So, know what you're looking for and be sure you ask it directly. People will be willing to answer it.

Step 5: Introduce the Survey

The fifth step in the process, once you have your questions developed, is to send a letter to the people you plan to survey. Or if you have a small number of customers, call them individually. Let them know why you are doing this; tell them that their feedback is important and describe what they will be asked. Essentially, you are requesting their permission to contact them. And it's just a nice touch, so that people aren't surprised when they receive a call from someone outside your organization or so, if you are mailing a survey, they'll be on the lookout for it. With the amount of junk mail and telemarketing phone calls, not to mention the relatively new "Do Not Call" list, the last thing you want to do is annoy your contacts with unexpected phone calls.

Also, be specific about how much time your survey will require. As a general rule, I would not request much more than 15 to 20 minutes of someone's time. If they want to speak longer, they can certainly do that, but be careful not to ask for too much time up front. One thing that is very interesting when you start this process is how many people are willing to share much more of their time once they start having the conversation. You can get some really incredible data once people start expressing their views. Susan tells me she has had respondents stay on the phone for half an hour or longer!

Step 6: Follow Up and Encourage Response

If a third party is conducting your survey, this is not necessary. However, if you have sent your survey via mail or e-mail, then you want to follow up with another e-mail or letter to say, "There's one more week until we begin to evaluate the responses. We'd appreciate your feedback. Please don't forget about it!" Because people do tend to put off surveys—particularly qualitative ones that may take some time—you often need to nudge.

Step 7: Express Your Gratitude in Writing

The next thing that you'd want to do is follow up with a thank-you. If any one of your customers takes the time to participate in a phone survey, a handwritten thank-you note is always appreciated and goes a long way to let them know that you appreciate the time they took to help you. Particularly when respondents stay on the phone for longer than the expected amount of time, you must express your appreciation. These touches are memorable and go a long way toward building strong customer loyalty.

Step 8: Collect and Organize Your Data

You need to keep in mind that once you ask for feedback, you own it. Once you have all of this, you need to make sure that you or the person you're working with analyzes the results, determines what it means to your business, and then creates an action list of changes you're going to make based on this feedback.

Step 9: Communicate Your Action Plan

The final step is perhaps the most important: showing your clients that you have taken their comments to heart. In addition to your personal thank-you notes, take the time to send a letter to your entire client base to say, "We did this survey. We received this kind of feedback. Thank you to everyone who participated and here's what were going to do as a result of this feedback." This gives you a chance to let people know that you are serious about your business, that you are going to make some critical changes, and then, over the course of the next six months to a year, report on your changes through regular progress reports. Clients—particularly new clients—love to see how your business is improving and like the fact that they had something to do with it.

Additional Benefits of Surveying

Besides improving your customer service, another strong advantage of conducting surveys is that you can use the process to update and segment your database and your reference list in your promotional kit or on your Website. The last thing you want to do is have people who aren't 100-percent satisfied with your product or service be a source on your reference list or your recommendation list if they're really not saying great things about your company. Also, you may come across people who are thrilled with your business who should be added to your reference list!

Finally, surveying offers you an opportunity to go back and revisit some satisfied (or dissatisfied) customers, to offer them an incentive to either continue to do business with you or to come back to you and possibly use you in a different way than they had in the past. As you can see, the key with any survey activity is to ACT based on the feedback you receive.

Creating Customers for Life

Believe me, I understand that overdelivering is not always easy. In fact, particularly when it comes to soliciting and responding to feedback, it's quite tough to hear an honest assessment of your value proposition. But this is a necessary component of building a highly successful business in today's world of instant feedback and virtually unlimited choices.

Your ultimate goal, however, makes it all worthwhile. The ultimate goal of all of our work in this book is to build *customers for life*. When you think about the lifetime value of keeping a client, once you have won their business, all of this work is extremely worthwhile. It is so much easier to retain the customer you have or to expand on the services or products you are selling than it is to go out and find a whole new customer. This is the focus of the final two chapters of this book. If you play your cards right and continue to overdeliver, you may never have to pitch another new client again. The business, as you will see, may just start pitching you.

One of my favorite—and simplest—stories of overdelivery found *me* at a seminar I gave at a local chamber of commerce event on Cape Cod, when an older man approached me with a binder in his hand. He said he was relieved that many of the things I had preached were things he was already doing—such as showing his potential customers his portfolio. His profession was not a graphic designer or architect, but rather a residential house painter.

He opened his book and I saw photographs of his loyal employees and painters, insurance riders, slews of handwritten testimonial and thank-you letters from satisfied clients, and before and after pictures of his work. I was so impressed by the way he documented his capabilities as a way of "pitching" himself to his clientele that I wanted to know more.

What was this man's reason for doing what so few people in his profession attempt to do—professionally sell their services to their prospects?

He said his secret formula was to have a person answer his phone, return calls promptly, show up when you say you will, leave behind something for them to remember you by (specifically, a press kit with testimonials and a magnet with his contact information), quote them an accurate price, do the job well when hired, and thank them at the end of the project by doing the unthinkable—sending them flowers as a thank-you gift.

I'm not sure what it's like to do business with local tradesmen in your area, but in my town, I'd be ready to hire a painter on the spot if he just showed up when he said he would—forget about the flowers!

The gentleman said this was his only form of marketing—all of his work came through referrals.

It really is so simple, isn't it? Answer your phone, schedule appointments, and show up. Have integrity with pricing and stay committed to what you said. Show up on the day you scheduled the job—do a good job and, finally, thank the client. So simple, but it's amazing how few people do it.

Imagine never having to "pitch" yourself again because, by overdelivering in each step of the process, you are selling yourself unbeknownst to anyone. Beats making cold calls, if you ask me!

Chapter 9

Take the Testimonial One Giant Step Farther: Create an Endorsement Campaign

The primary reason I am such a strong advocate of surveying customers is not that it provides an opportunity to recognize and fix problems (which, of course, it does), but because of the opportunity surveying provides for business owners to receive—and utilize—positive feedback. Happy clients are the secret weapon of marketing. But good feedback can't help you if it sits on a shelf in your office. You need to harness client satisfaction and put it to work for you.

Earlier in this book I talked a fair bit about the importance of buzz. Buzz—that intangible *feeling* of excitement or success—is extremely powerful and can drive sales and media attention for businesses of all shapes and sizes. This chapter takes buzz to the next level, showing you how to turn positive customer feedback and good word-of-mouth into specific, actionable marketing messages targeted to hand-picked prospects. Endorsement marketing appears near the end of *Perfecting Your Pitch* because you must master all of the earlier marketing and business development strategies in order to excel at endorsement marketing. As you will see, many of the skills developed in the preceding chapters will come in handy during your endorsement campaign.

Endorsements vs. Testimonials

Executed correctly, endorsements can be testimonials on steroids. A straight testimonial is when your client writes a letter directly to you, saying what a great job you've done. These are terrific to have, but an endorsement letter is much more powerful. My vision of an endorsement is when your best client writes a letter to specific prospects telling them about you and your wonderful product or service. The similarity between a testimonial and an endorsement is that both are written from your client's perspective and on their letterhead. The difference is that the endorsement letter is addressed directly to your prospects—and you orchestrate the process from start to finish.

Endorsements have a lot more power, because they give you unparalleled credibility. There is nothing like a third-party endorsement, especially from one high-level executive to another.

The 3-Tiered Endorsement Campaign

I will be honest with you: An endorsement campaign is a lot of work. You have to commit to the plan, because it involves a three-tiered process that must be fully thought through from the beginning. Following is a brief overview of the three tiers.

Tier 1: Identify Your Best Client (Your "Endorser") and Prepare Your Endorsement Letters

I've boiled down the endorsement letter-writing tier into seven action steps:

1. First, you need to identify your best client who would be willing to send a letter on your behalf. Many people are quite shy about asking a satisfied client to do this. If this is an issue for you, here are some points to keep in mind:

    ◪ Choose your endorser carefully. Select a client who has indicated his or her complete satisfaction with your services during a survey, in writing, or in conversation. Be sure that the endorser truly knows you and your product or service so that he or she can speak about you in detail. Ideally, you will want to ask someone with whom you have a long-standing relationship and a track record of results, rather than a new client.

◪ Recognize the endorsement campaign process as an opportunity to remind your best client about all the good that you've done for his or her company. When you ask a client to provide support for you, it reminds them of the success you have brought their way. Often the side benefit of an endorsement campaign is that you may win more business from the endorsing client!

◪ Assure your endorser that you will not "outgrow" their business by expanding your client base. In fact, just the opposite is true. No client wants you to have all of your eggs in his or her basket. Building a large client base helps strengthen your company, limit risk, and diversify and improve your product or service offerings.

◪ Endorsing you can also improve the reputation of your client. When you provide excellent products or services to the referral, your best client will receive as much of the praise as you will. Then, everyone wins.

◪ Show your gratitude often. A genuine request for help and support, followed by heartfelt thanks can go a long way toward building a strong bond between you and your client.

Once you become comfortable with the idea of asking your best client for an endorsement, what exactly are you asking? Ideally, you will write an endorsement letter and your client will agree to send it on his or her company letterhead. You want to do all the legwork for your client—and note that you should always offer to reimburse your client for the stationery and postage costs.

I recommend asking your best client in person or over the phone to perform this important service for you. Then, follow up with an e-mail message reviewing your request and the action steps to come.

2. Write the endorsement letter on your client's behalf. I would suggest that you use many bullet points and several facts and statistics about what results you've created for your client. Your goal with the endorsement letter is for your existing client to make a recommendation that your prospects can't refuse.

When you send the endorsement letter to your client to review, revise if necessary, and transfer to company letterhead, include some additional information or an example of your product to support the endorsement letter. For instance, when I asked Bruce Nelson, CEO of Staples, to write an endorsement letter on my behalf, I enclosed copies of my book *Off the Wall Marketing Ideas*. The letter said, "Nancy would be happy to meet with you in person or over the phone—here is her contact information—and here is a copy of her book as well." The book was a freebie that helped to build immediate goodwill.

The trick here is to provide additional information *of value*. I included a book, but you could send a copy of an article that you authored, reprints of publicity you've received, or anything that provides just a little bit more value. Generally speaking, I believe and have seen mounting evidence that longer letters sell more. I think two to three pages is sufficient—I wouldn't suggest anything longer than that, particularly if you are sending to busy CEOs, but more than one page shows substance.

Next, ask your client/endorser for his or her signature on a blank piece of paper, ideally in blue ink, so you can scan it into the document so it looks as though it's an original signature. This is very important, if you are planning to send the endorsement letter to a relatively large list of prospects or if you don't plan to send all of your letters at once. You don't want to bother your client every time you want to send a new endorsement letter to a particular prospect who may not have been on your original list.

3. Create a prospect list. This is a list of people to whom you would like to send your endorsement letter. Your list may include the prospect list you created at the beginning of this book, as well as other potential clients you have recently identified. At this point, you should be shooting for the top. The endorser's name on your letter can open doors you may not have been able to open previously.

   After you create your updated prospect list, show it to your client/endorser for approval. Let your endorser know that you will not send a letter to any prospect he or she is not comfortable contacting. Obviously, there should be no direct competitors of your endorser on the list! As a bonus, you may be pleasantly surprised that your client recommends people to add to your list or that the client has new information about a particular prospect you are targeting.

4. I always give my client the opportunity to have a final review and to give his or her approval of the letter so they can edit it, if they would like. If they want to edit the prospect list, I feel it is only fair to allow them to do this as well.

5. Graciously offer to return the favor. I told Bruce Nelson—and I meant it—that if there was anything he needed me to do for him, I would be happy to do it. And he did! About a month later he called me and said, "Okay, it's payback time. I want you to come to a political fundraiser at our offices and the ticket price is $1,000." Basically, you got a muffin, a cup of coffee, and a glass of orange juice for 1,000 bucks, but I did it because it was the right thing to do. I told him I would do something and be willing to return the favor. Besides, the fundraiser was a great networking experience for me! I was able to meet many people that I had not had the opportunity to meet before, and it was definitely something that I think Mr. Stemberg remembered and was grateful for. How ever you can thank your client for endorsing you, be ready, willing, and able to do it.

6. Collect the company letterhead or personalized stationery so that you can reproduce the letter and do the mailing yourself.

7. I highly recommend that you actually go to the town in which your client is based to mail the letters, because you want the post office insignia to have that town's postmark on it. This is kind of getting down to the real nitty-gritty level of detail, but these little things can make a big difference in the success of your endorsement campaign. I have a virtual assistant in Florida who is tapped into a network of virtual assistants in several cities who will mail letters for her. Think about friends or colleagues you know who might be willing to do a mail drop for you.

You also want to handwrite your prospects' names on the envelope or package and mail either Priority or First Class. I tested whether FedEx, UPS, or Airborne is more effective, and found that the response rate was almost the same as with the U.S. Postal Service. If your prospects are *Fortune* 1000 CEOs, note that all CEO mail ends up getting logged, which means it doesn't seem to matter by which method the mail is sent. This fact can save you a lot of money—don't waste your pennies on overnight mail that won't be opened for a week!

Sample Endorsement Letter for Financial Advisor

Dear [prospect's name]:

As the owner of **Impression Impact**, I'd like to pass along the name of a phenomenal financial advisor who has greatly helped me and my company. Carolyn Howard, the principal of **Pegaesus Advisors, Inc.**, located in Lexington, Massachusetts, delivers practical financial advice, gains the long-term trust of clients, and creates unique financial plans for a wide variety of small businesses and individuals.

Carolyn specifically helped my business by pointing out that I could receive a better healthcare program through my local Chamber of Commerce and showing me several business write-offs that I wasn't utilizing. Also, she had me sign up for U-promise, a Web location to register my credit card so that up to 10% of every purchase I made went directly to our oldest child's college fund. Another useful idea was to create a flexible spending account allowing my husband and me to contribute tax-free contributions to help cover our children's medical and dental expenses, daycare, and any qualified emergencies that may arise.

What sets Carolyn apart from other advisors is her ability to carefully listen to each person and discover what his or her needs are on an individual basis. She makes herself available for questions from clients and is glad to answer every type of query. Knowing how time-consuming financial planning is to most people, her planning services allow one to gain more control over a stressful area of modern life.

Carolyn tailors each financial plan to the unique needs and future plans of each company or individual. She does this by structuring plans to include low- or no-cost administration expenses, factoring in investment flexibility at institutional pricing, and continuing to educate clients regarding each step in the overall process. Carolyn has created a state-of-the-art plan administration—one that guarantees cost reduction at all levels.

Carolyn's services are valuable to her clients because she:

- □ Connects people to their money in ways which offer tangible results.
- □ Creates plans relating directly to the individual needs of each company or person.
- □ Assists small business owners in developing plans to prepare for long-term emergency situations.
- □ Finds numerous cost-cutting methods to save money for her clients.
- □ Retains clients by bringing a unique vision and strong emotional component to her financial plans.
- □ Believes planning requires consistency, quality, and communication, and delivers on all fronts.
- □ Understands why people stay with financial planners and gives true information about how her system employs innovative methods.

Carolyn says, "I offer plans that people feel are both practical and easy to understand. What small business executives require in financial matters is a partner, a guide, and an educator."

Carolyn delivers strategic, low-cost pension consulting and excels in helping clients connect their money to their lives. This area of expertise is particularly crucial for the executives of small companies. She first analyzes a business's current financial picture, returns with recommendations in line with short- and long-term goals, and offers insights into how they can implement innovative ideas into their financial lives. She targets specific areas, such as tax planning, so that one may allow for pretax dollars to pay for out-of-pocket medical expenses, childcare and eldercare, and she finds ways in which business owners can increase contributions to their plans.

One of Carolyn's unique methods is to charge a flat fee that she customizes for each client's planning needs. This fee gives them access to her company for one year, without additional costs. Carolyn put this method into practice because she noticed most people didn't implement financial plans they had signed up for, because additional costs were associated with the implementation process. A great many of her clients have come to her with incomplete plans. After people discover what the competition offers, most return to Carolyn, bringing with them a clearer understanding of both the commitment and the quality available at **Pegaesus Advisors**.

In addition to covering the entire spectrum of planning and investment consulting, Carolyn knows that modern consumers are savvy about exploring their financial options.

By being able to clearly communicate her financial knowledge and particular brand of planning, Carolyn assures each client and guides them with expertise.

Carolyn has been featured in **_The Boston Globe_** and has been quoted in **_The Wall Street Journal_**. Currently, she is a highly-regarded speaker for financial planning workshops and seminars.

Carolyn can be contacted at (781) 860-0410. She can also be reached via fax at (781) 860-0412. Her e-mail address is choward@pegaesusadvisors.com. Her Website is *www.pegaesusadvisors.com.* I hope you do connect with her. Carolyn has proven herself to be an astute and exceptional financial planner, and she is definitely worth getting to know.

Sincerely,

Nancy Michaels
Principal of Impression Impact

Disclaimer: Ms. Howard did not request an endorsement letter, but I was so impressed with her services that I wanted others to know of her and her company.

[Note: Only allow endorsers to include such a disclaimer if it is true. In some industries, such as financial services, this is required by law.]

Sample E-mail/Letter Confirming Process With Endorser

Dear [*prospect's name*],

Many thanks for your help on this.

As promised, I am attaching a Microsoft Excel spreadsheet of the companies I would like this letter to go out to, as well as a draft of the endorsement letter that you can certainly feel free to edit as you deem necessary.

If [the endorser] is willing to sign each of these on your letterhead, I would be very grateful. I am happy to cover any of the administrative costs surrounding this effort (such as letterhead, mailing labels, and so forth). I have a virtual assistant in Delray who will pick them up and mail them out from a nearby post office on Friday, if possible. I will follow up with two letters to this group of CEOs in the three weeks to follow and will keep you apprised of any and all responses I receive from [endorser]'s endorsement of my work.

Again, many thanks for your efforts and willingness to go to bat for me. I look forward to seeing you next week. Please know that I'm ready, willing, and able to return the favor when you need me. Please don't hesitate to call upon me.

Warmly,

[your name]

Tier 2: Follow-Up Letter From You

Once you have mailed your client endorsement letters to your prospect list, the next "tier" of the endorsement campaign is to send a follow-up letter from you. Before undertaking this next phase, be sure that you are prepared administratively and mentally to receive inquiries. You will hopefully find that someone who has received a recommendation about you from a trusted or impressive business associate has a strong willingness to meet, speak with you, or at least have additional information sent. It's always perceived differently than if you're trying to pitch yourself.

Two to three weeks after sending your client endorsement letters, send a letter on your company letterhead to that same list of prospects. This second letter is directly from you to your prospects. It is crucial that, at the beginning of the letter, you remind them of your client's generosity and willingness to send a letter on your behalf. This reminds them of where they might have heard about you.

Next, reiterate the points that were made in the client endorsement letter without being redundant. Remind your prospects of what it is that you did for that client. Show your track record of results.

In this follow-up letter, I recommend including a fax-back form— and don't forget to feature your fax number prominently on the form! (I know it sounds like I'm stating the obvious here, but this is a mistake I made once.) Of course, provide your phone number(s) and e-mail address as well, so the prospect can contact you however he or she desires.

I also recommend including two or three other testimonial letters or quotes from satisfied clients in this follow-up package. Additionally, you could offer a discount, a giveaway, or a coupon. This is also an opportunity to provide additional relevant information, such as an article you've authored, a tip sheet on your product or service, or something that is going to hopefully be more of a "keeper."

Sample Endorsement Follow-Up Letter #1

Dear [*prospect's name*]:

I am following up on Nancy Michaels's recent letter to you. My client, the president of Impression Impact, was gracious enough to endorse my work. I am indebted to her for her gesture.

Ms. Michaels explained the work I did for her and her business. She discussed the contributions I have made to her business and personal finances, including pointing out areas where she could save money, business write-offs, and a more cost-efficient healthcare program. As she stated in her letter, she believes that you personally or your business can benefit from my expertise as a Certified Financial Planner and Registered Investment Advisor.

I certainly hope that I'll be able to convince you of the same. That's my goal—which leads to my second reason for writing you.

I want to share a couple of ideas with you and propose a few ways in which Pegaesus Advisors can make a difference to you or your company's current and future financial state. I would be happy to meet with you over the phone for a brief conversation to learn more about your financial planning needs and/or send you an information package about my company for your review.

Briefly, there are several ways that Pegaesus Advisors can assist you or your business:

1. Creating a basic financial plan.
2. Estate planning.
3. Retirement planning, including company 401(k).
4. Long-term care planning.
5. Insurance planning.
6. Education planning.
7. Investment planning.
8. Portfolio analysis.
9. Cost basis analysis.
10. Investment policy statement.
11. Business planning.

Recently, I was a speaker for an Office Depot Web Café on "Financial Fitness for the New Year," including tax tips, planning for 2004, and 10 ways to save money today. You might be interested in the materials covered. If you would like to view the archived presentation, it is available anytime at *www.officedepot.com/webcafe*. Simply click on the archive tab at the top of the page and then choose to replay my presentation. I have included the top 10 points from the Web Café for you to review at your convenience—hopefully you will find them to be helpful.

[*Prospect's name*], I appreciate your time and look forward to working with you. You can call me directly anytime at 781-860-0410, or e-mail me at choward@pegaesusadvisors.com.

Best Regards,

Carolyn Howard, CFP

Tier 3: Final Follow-Up

Phase three of this endorsement campaign is the final letter from you to your prospect list—a final follow-up to people who have not responded after your client's letter and your first follow-up effort.

Keep in mind that you want to continue to be prepared to receive inquiries, and you obviously do not want to send additional follow-up information to people who have responded. If they've already called and inquired about your product or service, don't send them another letter! You should follow up more appropriately, with a phone call and/or meeting request.

For prospects who have not yet responded, I would suggest resending your client's original letter as a reminder, about two to three weeks later, with a note that reiterates how happy you are that your client was willing to do this for you. That way, if they missed it the first time and had no idea what you were talking about the second time, hopefully they will get it by the third try! You also want to update them on any additional news related to the success you've brought to your best client in connection with your product or service. Again, include a fax-back form. Finally, be willing to provide something else from you—this time it might be a press kit, a newsletter, or a postcard.

Sample Endorsement Follow-Up Letter #2

Dear [*prospect's name*]:

Several weeks ago Impression Impact president Nancy Michaels wrote to you about my work in creating successful financial plans and offering valuable financial and investment advice. I've attached a second copy of the letter for your convenience.

I followed up with a letter, but I realize that you must be extremely busy and thought I would contact you one more time.

As I said, I would welcome the opportunity to speak with you regarding the possibility of Pegaesus Advisors providing the following services:

1. Creating a basic financial plan.
2. Estate planning.
3. Retirement planning, including company 401(k).
4. Long-term care planning.
5. Insurance planning.
6. Education planning.
7. Investment planning.
8. Portfolio analysis.
9. Cost basis analysis.
10. Investment policy statement.
11. Business planning.

Money is an emotional issue. Given that, it is essential to have a trusting and close relationship with your planner. To give you a better idea of my work and my approach, I have enclosed an article I was quoted, in from *The Wall Street Journal*. This article demonstrates my personal approach to planning for each client and acknowledgment that financial issues affect all areas of your life. My goal is to help you to understand your financial situation and educate you about your options, as well as provide a framework to make the best choices possible.

Other articles and additional information about me and Pegaesus Advisors are available at *www.pegaesusadvisors.com.*

I look forward to discussing ways we might work together to maximize the financial well-being of you and/or your business. Please feel free to call me at 781-860-0410 anytime, or to e-mail me at choward@pegaesusadvisors.com.

Best Regards,

Carolyn Howard, CFP

At this point, you may also want to deepen your prospect list with some care. For instance, include the names of those not originally on your list—somebody's assistant or a person at another level of the company—in your database.

The final stage of the third tier of follow-up is to make personal phone calls to pursue prospects you have not heard from. This final level of connection may elicit even more information that you can use to pursue a prospect now or in the future. When I conducted my first endorsement campaign, I had various companies coming back to me with letters that the CEO might have passed down to somebody in his or her marketing department. I learned that they had a committee meeting or a committee formed specifically to handle their small business marketing initiatives. Everybody who was in that meeting was copied on the list. By following up by phone and learning this, I was able to greatly expand my database of prospects by including all of those people's names on my list.

Example of Endorsement Campaign Follow-Up Phone Call

Expert networker and author Diane Darling of Effective Networking, Inc., in Boston shares her follow-up script. Note how she keeps it short and to the point, but also injects her personality and the personality of her business.

Hi—I'm following up on the packet sent to you by [*sender's name*].

It had a reprint of a magazine article called "How to Work a Room" as well as a book called *The Networking Survival Guide.*

I'm the author, Diane Darling.

I wanted to walk my talk and network with you. I frequently tap into my network to help reporters find a source for their stories. If I can be a resource for you, I'd be happy to help.

If you have any questions about the book, of course I'm happy to talk to you about that as well. It's in its second printing and just came out in Korean.

I'll leave you my contact information—

My name again is Diane Darling.

The phone number is 617.305.2121.

E-mail is Diane@EffectiveNetworking.com.

You can also go to the Website for the book, *www.NetworkingSurvivalGuide.com.*

Thank you for your time!

Final Thoughts on the Endorsement Campaign Strategy: Just Do It!

I know that creating and executing an endorsement campaign can be administratively intense. I've gone through it several times—the research, requesting, stuffing, stamping, proofreading, resending, calling, and worrying. If you feel somewhat uncomfortable taking on an endorsement campaign, you are certainly not alone. A lot of people have difficulty with this. They are afraid of being rejected. They feel too modest. But here is the fact that trumps all fear and anxiety: There is *nothing* like the endorsement campaign for generating word-of-mouth referrals, which are the very best you can get. Endorsement campaigns can replace "cold" calling and pitching for the rest of your business career. In the next and final chapter, we will look at more ways to increase your visibility, in order to decrease your pitching time.

Chapter 10

Lifelong Marketing

Successful businesspeople know that marketing is a never-ending pursuit. Coca-Cola, Budweiser, M&M's, and McDonald's are extremely successful household names, but they all come up with new advertising and marketing campaigns on a continual basis to stay on top. You need to do this, too. No matter how successful you become and how many new business pitches you win, you can never stop marketing.

This chapter contains my best tips for employing strategic, creative marketing activities that will help you maintain and expand the success you have achieved thus far. As we discussed in the previous chapter, effective marketing strategies can result in new business knocking on your door, rather than the other way around.

While every business has different needs, I have designed the suggestions in this final chapter to be broad enough to adapt to virtually any product or service offering.

The Mantra of Marketing: VCR

Every morning, every business owner should wake up, stretch, and then repeat the following three words: *visibility*, *consistency*, and *repetition*. VCR is the foundation of any successful marketing strategy. You want to be visible in a very consistent way. Then you want to repeat that message over and over to your respective target markets or niche markets.

Utilizing a media mix—a variety of ways to communicate with your clients and prospects—will produce the best results. Using e-mail, direct mail, and publicity is a better combination than just one method of addressing your target market.

As you are planning your marketing strategy, always remember what has worked for you in the past. Did you do a newsletter that was very effective—in fact, so effective, that you ultimately stopped using it? Maybe it's time to bring it back to life again. Try to keep things simple and uncomplicated. This way, you'll be more likely to continue to pursue marketing activities that you enjoy and that have worked for you in the past.

As you read through the recommendations in this chapter, think about the marketing ideas you want to implement in your business. Determine how to accomplish these, assign each a date for completion, then work backward from your deadline. I recommend creating a marketing calendar to schedule your efforts in an organized way. A calendar can help you to effectively identify marketing opportunities throughout the year and execute your ideas in a less stressful and more proactive manner. If used well, it can be your map and guide to reach your marketing destination—on time and with great reward.

An example of a marketing effort for a retailer would be to send customers a Thanksgiving Day card about two weeks before the holiday shopping season. The retailer would have to get started on this project no later than September, in order to meet with a designer and hire administrative help to update the database program or list of contacts. By the time the cards are designed and printed, the mailing list updated, the envelopes addressed and stamped, and the cards mailed, holiday shopping season is just around the corner. By planning the mailing well ahead of time, the retailer will see faster and more significant results, with fewer headaches.

The Rules of 4 and 6

Exactly how much marketing is necessary? There's an 80/20 rule in business that I'm sure you've heard: We typically get 80 percent of our business from 20 percent of our customers. However, most of us market to all of our customers in the same way. The problem with this is that we spend considerably more (80 percent more, perhaps) than we need to and get fewer results than we'd expect. Just think: If we spent 80 percent of our marketing initiatives on the 20 percent that bring us the majority of our income, our business would expand accordingly.

I like to use a "Rule of 4" and "Rule of 6" when marketing my company or my consulting clients.

The Rule of 4 is that everybody in my database hears from me four times a year, or once per quarter. They might receive an offline newsletter twice a year and a postcard twice a year.

The Rule of 6 is that my A-list customers hear from me an additional two times per year. Usually the additional two communications are of a personal nature, such as birthday cards or handwritten notes.

You can certainly communicate with your database of contacts more than four or six times per year, such as through a regular e-zine, as I'll discuss in the following section, but I believe these are the minimum requirements for visibility. Another important aspect is that the Rules of 4 and 6 remind you that you should not market to everyone in the same way. While every customer and potential customer is important, some are clearly more valuable to you than others. Think about where the majority of your profits come from and market to those customers more frequently.

Perfect Your Online Presence

As I mentioned early in this book, every business needs an online presence. We are so lucky in this day and age to have the Internet, because it makes visibility so much less expensive and easy to update. Of course, the challenge of the Internet is its vastness. How do you entice prospects and customers to visit your Website, when there are billions of pages of information at their fingertips? You cannot rely on people to find you; you have to tap on their shoulders and give them compelling reasons to visit and revisit your Website. Enter the e-zine.

E-zines are familiar to most people at this point, but I am surprised at how few business owners employ them effectively. E-zines are online newsletters that can be as simple as text newsletters or as elaborate as short films. What type of e-zine you choose will depend on your business, but the act of communicating with your customers via a formalized electronic communication can rarely fail you. Companies with a diverse clientele, from K-Mart to Kate Spade, employ various forms of e-zines to keep in touch with their customers and draw in more sales.

Here are some tips for creating and maintaining a successful e-zine for your business needs:

- **Build a strong database.** To create a distribution list for your e-zine, find creative ways to ask your prospects, customers, media contacts, and other business contacts to "opt in" to your online communication. If you are subscribed to my Impression Impact e-zine, you have either come to my site and signed up (I recommend a pop-up sign-up box that visitors see when they arrive on the homepage of your Website) or you have received something from me with a link that you might have clicked on and then signed up for it. You can also collect business cards at conferences where you speak or exhibit. Just be sure to clearly mark on your fish bowl or collection box that, by providing their business cards, people understand that they will receive communication from you.

   Do not be discouraged if your database is small at the beginning. I admit that, when I started my business, my database consisted entirely of friends and family. But you have to start somewhere, so dive in and don't worry.

- **Be aware of legal issues.** You have to be very careful about spam and junk mail issues. You absolutely cannot send e-mail messages to people who have not agreed to receive them and you must include an "unsubscribe" option in every communication. So I have in my e-zine what I call an opt-in e-zine list or an opt-in online database, which means that everyone has given me permission to be put on that list.

- **Find an e-zine vendor to manage the process.** Once your database includes more than a few dozen people, it is in your best interest to use an outside vendor to manager the distribution of your e-zine. This does not need to be expensive (the cost is usually based on how many people are on your distribution list) and many vendors provide this service to small business owners. I have a relationship with a company called Constant Contact, which is a great e-zine system. With the company's do-it-yourself e-mail marketing program, you can manage your e-mail lists and create eye-catching HTML e-newsletters, customized with your logo and other materials. You even have the ability to track results of your e-mail campaigns, including open and click-through rates. Constant Contact offers a 60-day free trial, after which its services are very affordable.

E-zine Example #1

Michaels on Marketing

By Nancy Michaels

Michaels on Marketing is a monthly publication devoted to helping you achieve your marketing goals creatively and cost-effectively.

Please forward this newsletter to friends and colleagues who might be interested!

In This Issue:

- Upcoming Office Depot's Web cafe series

- Office Depot's Success Strategies Conference

Subscribe

Visit
Impression Impact

Feedback

Impression Impact

impressionimpact.com

(781) 860.8881

Nancy Michaels

Happy New Year to all –

I wanted you to be aware of two exciting events that are coming up.

1. Office Depot's Web Café series with a line-up that will knock your socks off! Go to www.officedepot.com/promo/webcafe for details and to sign up. We have Jay Abraham, Marketing Guru to kick the event off on Tuesday, January 13th from 4 – 5 pm EST.

2. Office Depot's Success Strategies Conference (download the attached pdf for details) in February, where you'll hear Katie Couric, Hillary Rodham Clinton, and many other wonderful speakers.

And finally, don't forget to mark your calendar for January 22rd, Chinese New Year, the Year of the Monkey. Stay tuned to my Top 10 List for the Chinese New Year.

Best,

Nancy

Office DEPOT.
What you need. What you need to know.

To unsubscribe from *Michaels on Marketing*, simply send a blank e-mail with a REMOVE in the subject line to:

enewsletter@impressionimpact.com

- **Develop an e-zine content strategy.** People will only read your e-zine if you are providing valuable content that is easy to digest on a computer screen. I always have a top-10 list, which is one effective way to stand out in people's minds because everybody has time to read 10quick ideas. When an e-zine is very dense in text, it is not as likely that people will go through and read every word. You want to make it fun and useful to your readers, but also somewhat of an easy read.

E-zine Example #2

WH Cornerstone Investments Newsletter

Turning your paycheck into a playcheck TM   June 2004

In this issue

Markets Watch June 30—Caution Reigns as Mid-Year Approaches

Medicare Act of 2003

Money and Marriage

Inheriting a Spouse's IRA

Mutual Funds Still Offer Benefits

Unique Advantages of Annuities

Dear Paula,

Summer is fast approaching; at least the calendar says so. Before all the BBQ's and boat trips begin take a moment to get caught up on the latest in financial planning. The June 14 edition of Mass High Tech will feature an article written by our very own Bill Harris. The article is called The Real Estate IRA and will appear in the finance section. http://www.masshightech.com/

Time to share. Create a buzz. The Alden House is a Window on the Past. America's first couple, John and Priscilla Alden, made their home in Duxbury after leaving Plimouth Plantation. The present Alden House was built in 1657 and is owned by the Alden Kindred of America. The house covers over 300 years of history and is an amazing treasure. Stop on by for a glimpse through a Window on the Past. For more information visit: http://www.alden.org.

Back Roads of the South Shore

Markets Watch June 30—Caution Reigns as Mid-Year Approaches

Note June 30 on your calendar. Not only is this the midpoint of the year and the end of the second fiscal quarter, but several other significant events will occur that may impact investors. Here's a capsule summary of the events culminating on June 30 that could have a significant impact on the economy in the months to come.

The United States—or, more specifically, the U.S.-led Coalition of Provisional Authority (CPA)—has established June 30 as its deadline to hand over sovereignty in Iraq to a newly established interim government. The CPA expects elections to be held before the end of the year, or shortly thereafter, in conjunction with the writing of a new Iraqi

- **Medicare Act of 2003**

The Medicare Prescription Drug, Improvement, and Modernization Act of 2003 represents the largest expansion in the Medicare health entitlement program since it was enacted in 1965. Three main provisions will affect most families.

Prescription Drug Savings—A prescription drug benefit will be offered to all 40 million seniors and disabled Americans in Medicare. After beneficiaries pay a $35 monthly premium and a $250 annual deductible, the benefit will cover 75 percent of the cost of each person's prescription drugs, up to $2,250 per year. Seniors will have to pay all their own drug costs between $2,250 and $5,100; after costs reach the $5,100 level, catastrophic coverage kicks in, paying 95 percent of drug costs. The drug benefit program doesn't begin until 2006. In the meantime, seniors

Read on the Medicare Act of 2003...

- **Money and Marriage**

Recent research has revealed some fundamental differences in the way men and women typically invest. This may explain why an estimated 30% of married couples have never discussed their finances.

Instead of risking a disagreement, many couples leave money matters in the hands of one partner, but a sudden disability, death, or divorce could leave the uninformed spouse in a difficult spot.

Full Story about Money and Marriage...

constitution. In the second quarter, Frank Russell Company, the prominent investment services firm, "reconstitutes" its 21 U.S. equity indexes as part of an annual process to accurately reflect stock market activity and performance. More than $350 billion is invested in mutual funds modeling the Russell indexes, which rank the 3,000 largest U.S. companies by market capitalization. The reranked indexes will take effect after June 30.

In the second quarter, Frank Russell Company, the prominent investment services firm, "reconstitutes" its 21 U.S. equity indexes as part of an annual process to accurately reflect stock market activity and performance. More than $350 billion is invested in mutual funds modeling the Russell indexes, which rank the 3,000 largest U.S. companies by market capitalization. The reranked indexes will take effect after June 30.

● Inheriting a Spouse's IRA

When a spouse dies, the survivor is often forced to make a number of financial decisions. If no plan is in place, some of the decisions may be uncomfortable. Worse, making a mistake can result in tax penalties, lost value, and a potentially higher tax burden. Even though the IRS issued rules in 2001 that make it easier for a surviving spouse to inherit an IRA, it is still critical to make knowledgeable decisions because they could have far-reaching consequences. Consider what can happen to an IRA left to a spouse as sole beneficiary.

Two Options to Consider—Leave the account in the deceased spouse's name. With this option, you are still required to take minimum distributions (either based on your single life expectancy or the year in which the IRA owner would have reached age 70½). Failing to take required minimum distributions could result in a penalty of 50 percent of the amount you should have withdrawn. Of course, if you don't change the account ownership to your name, the beneficiary of the account will be the contingent second beneficiary designated by the deceased spouse, not necessarily someone you name.

Read on to learn more about Inheriting a Spouse's IRA...

● Mutual Funds Still Offer Benefits

In 2003, a series of scandals erupted in the mutual fund industry that grabbed headlines for months. Regulators reacted swiftly by proposing new rules and pursuing offenders. Although the scandal was widely publicized, the affected companies represented a minority in the universe of mutual funds. It's important to note that there are thousands of mutual funds for investors to choose from today.

Wall Street expects interest rates to increase this summer for the first time in four years, possibly when Federal Reserve policymakers meet on June 29 and 30. The Fed is expected to raise rates in an effort to rein in inflationary forces caused by the strongest economic growth in five years. U.S. treasurys have already reacted. By mid May, yields on the benchmark 10-year Treasury note were averaging 4.75%, up from 3.75% six weeks earlier.

To read the full article online....

The fact is, mutual funds remain extremely popular. In 2003, net inflows to long-term mutual funds grew by 79 percent from 2002. In December 2003, after the scandal had reached a crescendo, more than $15 billion of new money flowed into long-term funds (stock, bond, and hybrid funds). Why are investors sticking with mutual funds? It could be because they continue to offer benefits that are important to investors.

More on Mutual Funds...

● Unique Advantages of Annuities

When markets are volatile, people may look for stability. When markets are hot, people may seek growth potential. Annuities may help answer both strategies.

During 2002, people poured about $168 billion into individual annuities—an increase of 19 percent over the prior year. An annuity is basically a contract with an insurance company. In exchange for your payments—made over time or in a lump sum—the insurance company agrees to pay you future income for a set number of years in retirement. Annuities have some very attractive features.

Read on to learn more about Annuities...

● Back Roads of the South Shore

Hidden History from Boston to Plymouth Backroads of the South Shore is a collaborative project of thirteen leading historic sites in eight towns along the south shore of Massachusetts. The group is dedicated to creating an awareness of the area's historic gems and celebrating the heritage and spirit of the region.

Click here to learn more about these treasures

| email us |
| :: visit our site |
| phone: 781.934.9154 |

Additional Web Marketing Strategies for Maximum VCR

Here are some additional Web strategies employed by other business owners to maximize their VCR:

- **Autoresponders.** When someone visits your Website and takes the time to send a comment or request information, it is a smart idea to let them know their communication has not fallen into the black hole of the World Wide Web. When someone signs up for something on my Website, they receive an auto response, which is an immediate e-mail message confirming that I have received his or her message.

  Third-party vendors also exist to provide and manager auto response messages for your Website. There is a company called 1ShoppingCart.com, for instance, that sets up many autoresponders. I use this company for the e-commerce portion of my Website. If somebody buys a product of mine, they will automatically receive a series of auto responses, thanking them and perhaps providing additional information about that product or another product that they haven't received but might interest them, based on the other product they purchased. This helps to provide added value and keep my name in front of my clientele.

- **Free reports.** You might also want to offer a free report or some other additional information that provides value to a site visitor immediately. Perhaps you might offer a top-10 list of tips for people in your industry or a white paper on an important topic. Be sure the free report provides just enough value to pique someone's interest to learn more about you and your business. Do not give too much for free!

- **Tell-a-friend.** When my friend Jane forwarded the tell-a-friend message to me from the Canyon Ranch Website, I was impressed from a marketing standpoint *and* I immediately signed up to join Jane and her daughter at Canyon Ranch for the weekend. Whenever you are promoting an event, new product launch, or any information about your products or services, add a button or forwarding function to make it easy for someone to forward the information to a friend. This strategy has proved very successful not only for businesses, but also for issues-based communication, such as with non-profit organizations and political campaigns.

- **Translate your site to reach mulitcultural markets.** If you have a wide client base or an active strategy to reach ethnic markets, you should consider translating your Website into another language. Fran Ruiz, an entrepreneur participating in one of my teleclasses, told me that clients have found her because her Website has a Spanish language version. "They've seen my site listed in the business resources—it's like the Yellow Pages, but online," she told me excitedly. "They've seen it in Spanish, and they've said, 'We called you because it says that you speak Spanish. Your site, your reference, was in Spanish.'"

  Can you reach out to diverse markets to expand your client base? Office Depot has a Spanish Website. They have hired Annette Taddeo and her company, Language Speak, to translate for them.

- **Host an online contest.** I've seen clients use various contests on their Websites so that people who enter also sign up for the e-mail list. The sign-up form can also ask for information such as a birthday, in order to join a "birthday club," for example. You can then send out monthly reminders that "Your birthday is coming up" or "Your wife's birthday is coming up," along with a coupon, as a special incentive. You might consider this strategy, especially if your company produces a product or service that someone would give as a gift. Or if you provide insurance or financial services, you might tie your marketing campaigns to financial strategies that correspond to various stages of life.

  I have found a way to use this strategy in my marketing consulting business. I ask Website visitors and clients for their birthdays and their bosses' birthdays. The results have been unbelievable. I will call people and leave a message for them first thing in the morning on their birthday and they cannot believe that I'm doing that. In fact, people will say, "My mother hasn't called me yet. I can't believe that you have!" These things really matter to people and show that you are thinking of them.

Direct Mail

Yes, Internet marketing is absolutely essential in this day and age. But direct mail is still holding its own. Letters, packages, postcards, and folders sent from your business to a target audience can be a productive form of marketing. But how can you make your package stand out like a big fish in a sea of junk mail? If you're anything like me, I bet you open your mail over the garbage can.

Will your direct mail piece make it past the wastebasket and onto the right person's desk? More important still, will it be on top of the stack to be opened? And most importantly, will the recipient become a new or repeat customer? The key is an attention-getting design that commands notice. To this end, I present my "10 Commandments" of direct mail—the do's and don'ts culled from some of my favorite marketing gurus—that can help your mailing get the attention and action it deserves.

I. Thou Shalt Have a Creative Concept

The most important thing is to make your direct mail piece stand out. But first you need to understand your product in terms of how it could be promoted. Good advertising copywriters typically use thesauri, dictionaries, or their own imagination to come up with key words and phrases that describe or are associated with the products or services they will be promoting.

You never know which everyday ideas will lead to inspiration. Sheree Clark, co-owner of Sayles Graphic Design, in Des Moines, Iowa, and author of *Creative Direct Mail Design* (Rockport Publishers, 1995), practices what she and her partner, John Sayles, preach. One of the most creative mailings to promote their services is a matchbook design that reads: "In the dark about how to set your business on fire?" The copy goes on to discuss "sizzling concepts" and "smokin' design." The reply card, to be checked off by the recipient, says, "Yes, I have a burning desire to know more."

Even a small business can reap big benefits and project a larger, more established image by carefully investing in creative and customized promotional gifts. To keep costs down, limit the number of items you mail and develop a relationship with an advertising specialty company whose products are affordable and complement your direct-mail pieces.

Of course, not every mailing requires an accompanying product. A good idea, combined with attention-getting copy, visually interesting graphics, and eye-catching colors (such as yellow and red), go a long way toward making your direct mail noticeable.

II. Thou Shalt Use AIDA

The "Rule of AIDA" is one of the most important things to remember, says Joan Throckmorton, who teaches seminars on direct mail for the New York City-based Direct Marketing Association. In her book *Winning Direct Response Advertising* (Prentice Hall, 1986), Throckmorton explains that smart direct mail practitioners always use AIDA—an acronym for Attract Attention, Arouse Interest, Stimulate Desire, and Call for Action.

AIDA words include *new*, to attract attention; *limited quantities*, to arouse interest; *exclusive*, to stimulate desire and *order now*, with a toll-free number, to effectively call for action.

III. Thou Shalt Write Titillating Copy

What attention-getting words work best? In their book, *The Do-It-Yourself Direct-Mail Handbook* (Raphel Publishing, 1992), authors Murray Raphel and Ken Erdman say that *free* is the magic word. Other words that evoke positive responses include *new, now, win, guarantee, you, easy,* and *breakthrough*.

There are times when full headlines, not just words, are needed. Effective headlines always promise a benefit, say Raphel and Erdman ("How to Lose 10 Pounds in 10 Days"), and provoke curiosity ("How to Look Younger in 14 Days"). Your headlines should also be believable, easy to understand, and offer something of value ("How to Produce Quick Meals in 15 Minutes").

Another rule of thumb for attention-getting copy, Throckmorton says, is to use short sentences. This style conveys your message directly and concisely. Use dashes and ellipses instead of semicolons. Seek rhythm in your copy. Read your text aloud and make sure it "sings."

IV. Thou Shalt Write Effective Letters

The headline is an important component of direct mail. This often takes the form of the Johnson Box, where important copy is set off by lines or asterisks and placed above the salutation. The box reveals the major points of your offer. For example: "Now, for the First time, an Exclusive Charter Opportunity for Concord Residents to Try Slim-Trim for Free!"

After the headline, the second most important thing in a direct mail letter is the postscript (PS)—a restatement at the bottom of the letter of your fabulous offer in the Johnson Box.

Effective letters also offer readers a chance to become involved—for instance, by peeling off a special label or pasting in a word. Throckmorton says that these devices can increase your response, because humans enjoy such interactive acts.

V. Thou Shalt Use Different Formats

If everyone's direct mail piece was a letter, would any stand out? To add novelty to a mailing, consider other formats:

- **Postcards** offer three distinct advantages. They're cheaper than first-class letters, they don't need to be opened, and they are a quick read. One way to make yours a keeper is by providing valuable information that compels the recipient to hold onto it. For example, a pediatrician could list phone numbers of police, fire, ambulance, and hospitals along with his or her phone number.

Once, Twice, Three Times a Postcard

Ask Patricia Davis, of Albuquerque, New Mexico, if she understands the power of three, when it comes to direct mail, and she'll be selling you on the concept. Patricia runs a commercial cleaning company and utilizes door-to-door canvassing and direct mail as her primary marketing strategy. She knows the advertising rule of thumb that it takes at least six impressions before your prospect understands what it is that you are attempting to sell him or her. Patricia places higher power on three consecutive interactions within a matter of weeks, and I agree.

First, her savvy designer, Rosalie Huang, has utilized Patricia's personality, good humor, and excellent business sense by making her the icon of her business identity. Combining a woman with short black hair and spunky style as the logo for the company and great copywriting by Dave Bexfield, the impression she leaves is a memorable one.

Patricia identifies her target market of commercial buildings in need of cleaning, and knocks on their door to speak with the owners of the companies or the office managers whose businesses reside in these buildings. She has a brief chat with them, leaves an off-sized postcard that describes her services and shows her squirting a spray bottle of cleaning solution, surrounded by a heap of other supplies.

Then, a week later, she sends out a second postcard—one that has a drawing of herself holding a toilet brush that reads, "Naturally, we brush daily," answering that age-old question, "How often will you clean the toilets?"

Cleverly, she sends out a third postcard the following week that depicts her kissing a squeegee and reads, "We'd like to be your main squeegee." In a low-threat, highly memorable way, she's had a face-to-face contact with a prospect and has followed up and creatively and cost-effectively answered the two most important questions a prospect would want to know before hiring a cleaning company: How often will you clean the toilets, and will you do the windows?

The sequence of sending these highly targeted pieces out within a certain amount of time yields significantly greater rewards than spreading your direct mail efforts over weeks, or even worse, months.

■ **Invitations** make the recipient feel wanted. An invitation will almost surely be opened, especially if it is hand-addressed and looks like it came from an individual, not a business. If feasible, hire a calligrapher or a professional who uses a computer calligraphy machine. Use stamps related to your company; for instance, Elvis stamps, if you own a music store, or breast cancer awareness stamps, if the majority of your customers are women.

■ **Calendars** have a good chance of being displayed. At my office we receive great calendars from a graphic design company that include marketing quotes for every day. Not only do they sit on our desks, but they are reminders of this small design house.

VI. Thou Shalt Have a Good Offer

Make an offer so good that your customers simply can't refuse. Find out what they want and offer it to them. Furthermore, it's smart to make a second free offer that piggybacks on the first. For example, a luggage store could offer a piece of luggage that comes with a travel pillow. Raphel and Erdman call this "the psychology of the second interest."

VII. Thou Shalt Mail Intriguing Envelopes

Make your envelopes look as if they were sent from a personal friend. If you have targeted your list, you may be able to afford to use stamps instead of using bulk-rate postage meter. Handwriting the addresses is a nice touch, but be sure to use recipients' names instead of "current resident."

Savvy direct marketers put "teasers" on their envelopes—intriguing messages in the lower left-hand corner. Serge Safar, owner of Safar Coiffure, a leading Boston hair Salon, got the attention of the beauty editors of *Allure, Vogue, Harper's Bazaar,* and other national publications when he mailed a press release describing how coffee could temporarily color your hair. The envelope's teaser read, "Discover how to perk up your hair with coffee." Safar also enclosed microwaveable coffee packets.

White or manila envelopes are borrrrring! Use colored envelopes to match your corporate colors or direct mail design concept. When you follow up by phone you can say, "It's in the purple envelope." As I mentioned earlier, The Cloth Envelope Company provides a unique alternative as well.

VIII. Thou Shalt Remain Visible

Consider a two- or three-part mailing. In his book *Streetfighter Marketing* (Lexington books, 1995), Jeff Slutsky cites two mailings from a Realtor. The first was an ordinary postcard, offering a free home warranty if you listed or purchased a home with the firm. The second mailing was an envelope containing a crumpled and flattened version of the first postcard attached to a note that read, "Please don't throw this out again." According to Slutsky, the response from recipients was, "How did this guy get back the postcard we trashed?" This mailing even inspired an article in his local newspaper.

IX. Thou Shalt Make It Easy for the Reader to Reply

Let's face it, most people are just too busy to reply to every direct mail piece, so essentially, you have to do it for them. Use a business reply card, coupon, toll-free number, or fax number; use whatever you have to get them to respond in one single step. As an incentive, you can offer a free gift in exchange for their response. Remember, the response rate will be higher if you give customers several ways to respond.

X. Thou Shalt Find Your Audience

As I have discussed in earlier chapters, your direct mailing is only as good as the database you mail it to. If you are not receiving the response you desire from the database you have so carefully cultivated, you may need to rethink your strategy. Perhaps the most obvious and strenuous test you can perform on a direct mail piece is to pay attention to the mailings you yourself open. Get in tune with the effective attention-getting features you see, and soon you'll have your own direct mail "commandments" to add to my list.

Celebrate a Nontraditional Holiday

One of my favorite marketing strategies is to find an unconventional holiday to celebrate with a card or small gift for your contacts— consider it a clever variation on direct mail. My company, Impression Impact, sends Chinese New Year cards and gifts to our clients and colleagues (in honor of my two adopted Chinese daughters). The Women's Business Enterprise National Council (WBENC) sends Valentine's Day wishes to those in its database. I have seen other businesspeople celebrate such events as the Super Bowl, Independence Day, and Halloween. Think about a holiday you can use not only to keep in touch with a particular prospect, but also to maintain contact with other people in your network.

For some ideas, you might want to check out *Gourmet Retailer* magazine, which is retail-focused but valuable to anyone for its monthly promotional calendar. From this publication, I have learned about such events as National Diet Month (January—for New Year's resolutions, of course!), National Oatmeal Month, National Booklet Month, Soup Month, National Gourmet Coffee Month, Bread Baking Machine Month, National Hot Tea Month, Elvis Presley's birthday, and many, many more.

One golden marketing opportunity that is unique to you and only you is to celebrate the anniversary of your business. I love a story I came across in the MarketingProfs.com online newsletter about Kerstin and Spencer Block, founders of Buffalo Exchange, in Tucson, Arizona. To celebrate the 30th anniversary of their fashion retail chain, they planned a 30-city tour. The tour transportation is a "retro-style" trailer from which they gave away T-shirts and coupons to their customers. The business owners also created photo boards and slide shows about their company's three decades in business. What can you do to celebrate your business anniversary in a way that is consistent with your brand and clientele?

Get a Gimmick

One of the reasons I like the story of Buffalo Exchange is because it reflects the personalities and products of the company's owners. While every business does not need cute giveaways or wild parties, I do think that most businesses can benefit from an appropriate and genuine gimmick that gives people that extra push to learn more about you and your products or services. Here are some fun examples that have generated real business results:

> "At the major trade show for the pet industry, the APPMA Show, I had on a bright colored outfit with fishing scenes and fish on it. It was quite loud. I also wore

shoes with fish and I walked around the show (when not at my booth) carrying a long bamboo fishing pole with a 2 oz. package of my DogNip Catch of the Day treats hanging from it. When asked what I had caught, I replied, 'Catch of the Day 100% REAL fish dog treats and Salmon Oil that makes every meal a treat and pumps on the nutritional benefits of Omega fatty acids.' People smiled at my whole-hearted confidence in my product line and my clever presentation."

—Debbie Claypool, DogNip Brand Inc.,
Palm Beach Gardens, Florida

McDonnell, Levine and Jenkins, an accounting firm in Boston, blends its Jewish and Irish heritages to retain clients: Every St. Patrick's Day it presents clients with green bagels!

Become a Published Expert in Your Field

Another ongoing marketing activity is to submit articles for publication in your industry. You do not have to get published in *The Wall Street Journal*—write for your local newspaper or the newsletter or Website of an association you belong to. Offer yourself as an expert for writers to interview as well; journalists are often happy to have a variety of experts in their Rolodexes who are willing to speak on a particular topic when a story arises. Whenever you do publish an article or appear as a quoted expert, be sure to request or buy additional copies of the publication and include them in your promotional kit as well as post electronic versions on your Website. Being mentioned in print can build your credibility enormously in your industry and community.

I think it is easiest to start off in your local hometown and try to generate publicity from journalists who cover your local business market. This was my strategy. I began by submitting marketing articles, for free, to a small local newspaper, because I knew the editor. From that experience, I had a few clips that I could send out, and this led to a few assignments to write for the *Boston Business Journal*, which was a little bit bigger than my local paper. So I wrote for that publication for a while.

Then, I started to have enough clips to send out to other larger magazines, and now I get hired to write for national publications such as *U.S. News & World Report* and *Entrepreneur*. It is all a process of building and growing your experience, exposure, and contacts. If you do not love to write, you can hire a freelance writer or ghostwriter to interview you for a story and then do the majority of the writing for you.

Remember to include media contacts in your database so they are up-to-date on your business. An editor may notice something in a mailing or e-zine that he or she thinks is newsworthy and hire you to write the piece!

Public Speaking Is Marketing

While it is extremely important to communicate with your clients and prospects in writing, nothing beats the connection of face-to-face interaction. I highly recommend that all business owners speak in public as frequently as possible. Speak at your local chamber of commerce or Rotary Club (note that Rotary Clubs meet weekly, so they are always looking for high-quality speakers) or anywhere that you can get some practice getting in front of an audience and telling your story.

Many business owners ask me whether or not they can charge for speaking to audiences. This depends on the nature of your business, the nature of your audience, and the topic about which you are speaking (and, of course, if you are a businessperson who makes a living as a professional speaker). Once I had been speaking in public for several years, I decided that I could not afford the time away from my business unless I received *something* in return. I decided if an organization could not pay me to speak that I would say, "Well, I really need to have the database of attendees." So I would collect business cards from members of the audience and tell them they would be added to my database. A nice way to do this is to raffle off something (such as one of your products or a gift certificate for your services) by collecting business cards from the audience and drawing one.

Teach

Education is another creative approach to marketing. Teach an adult education class—you can get some additional speaking exposure and probably clients from among your students or fellow faculty members. This is where I started doing a lot of speaking when I first got started in my business. You can also take some classes to improve your skills in certain areas and network with your classmates and teachers.

Keep Building (and Organizing) Your Contacts

The more people you know, the more people who know you. At every stage of business development you must continue to expand your network and maintain connection with the people you meet. Although it sounds mundane, keeping your database clean and updated without duplications and mistakes is a crucial element of marketing. Specifically:

- Be sure to find a database management system that works for your business and that you understand inside and out. These days, databases can arrange information in a variety of ways, print mailing labels, categorize by virtually any topic of information, and perform countless other tasks that can save you time and money. If you do not know all there is to know about your database program, hire an intern or a professional consultant to learn the program and teach you the ropes. Most programs also offer online learning tutorials so, if you prefer, you can learn the program late at night or early in the morning in the privacy of your office or home.

- Regularly clean your database. Again, hire an intern or perhaps a virtual assistant, to clean your database and check for duplications, mistakes, and interesting nuggets of information that you don't have time to find (for example, two of your prospects are married or you have 10 contacts at the same corporation). Perform this cleaning regularly—at least once per quarter—but always after you have sent a large mailing and received return mail with bad addresses or notices of address changes and mail forwarding.

- Take advantage of every opportunity to build your database. I have already mentioned collecting information on your Website and during public speaking events, but think also about collecting information from anyone who calls your office. Whenever someone new calls your office, ask if you may take down his or her information and add that person to your database. If you have an assistant or receptionist who answers your phone, train him or her to collect this information. All of these additional names add up, and you never know where a new client may hear about you.

Give Back

I began this book with the story of spending $1,050 on lunch with Office Depot CEO Bruce Nelson. Yes, I bought the lunch as a chance to pitch a business idea to my dream prospect, but there was another reason: The money was going to charity. I'd like to return to this element of the story to talk about what I consider to be one of the most vital components of business citizenship today: giving back. I have always been drawn to the concept of tithing—voluntarily giving 10 percent of your income to charity. While I believe that the percentage of your profits you donate to charity is entirely up to you, I believe it is imperative for successful businesspeople to do good along with doing well financially. One of my inspirations in this area is Mary Lou Andre, a nationally recognized wardrobe consultant, speaker, and author of *Ready to Wear: An Expert's Guide to Choosing and Using Your Wardrobe* (Perigee, 2004). Because Mary Lou is in the fashion business, she has created the concept of "fashionable giving" for her company's charitable endeavors, which have always been an essential component of her business success.

Mary Lou says, "When you give, you get back much more than you ever give away." Among her charitable endeavors is support for the National Multiple Sclerosis Society Central New England Chapter—a commitment based on very personal reasons. When Mary Lou was reacquainted with a childhood friend in September 1999, she was stunned to see first-hand the devastating effects of multiple sclerosis (MS) on such a young woman. When she was told that 78 percent of all people affected by MS are, in fact, women and that most are diagnosed between the ages of 28 and 40, it was easy for her to team up with Karen to create and cochair a fashion show fundraiser, "Dressing Well—An Evening to Benefit MS." This three-year initiative concluded in October 2003 and raised a total of $215,000.

Mary Lou shares some of her valuable advice for making charity work a component of your business:

Q: What are the professional and personal benefits of giving back?

A: Fashion and fund-raising go hand in hand, as there are many fashion shows that benefit charities, so it made sense for me to combine these areas in my business. Overall, we have helped to create a community of giving—I find that most people want to give back but they don't know how, so we make it easy for people to get involved. My employees and clients feel really good when they get involved.

I included community relations in my business plan when I formed my company. Even though I couldn't afford to write a check when I first started, it was always part of my vision to be a civic-minded company. The return on investment has been incredible. Some of the benefits include:

- Involving clients as sponsors and guests at VIP events—they truly appreciate the opportunity to give back in a meaningful way.

- Working with existing vendors to further strengthen our relationship and also trying out new partnerships.

- Strengthening my brand with other organizations that take part in charitable events in my community—people I may not have met otherwise.

- Receiving increased media exposure ties to charitable work and special events.

- Involvement in charity events is another news item about my business to share with people, to keep my company fresh in their minds.

- Really making a difference and feeling good about it.

Q: Are there any potential drawbacks to including charity work as part of your business?

A: Remember that you are still a business owner, so your charity work must fit with your other marketing strategies and your business plan. You can only take on so many projects at a time and still run a profitable business! Strike a balance and be careful not to spend too much time on your charity work. Entrepreneurs don't have a lot of time so we have to focus.

Q: What tips would you offer a business owner who wants to become more involved in charitable work and cause marketing?

A: Be sure to promote your work to maximize the exposure of the charity and to maximize the benefit to your company's efforts. Here are some specific suggestions:

◪ Support charities that are meaningful to you personally, professionally, or both. The majority of my clients are women, so I work with charities such as the MS Society and Dress for Success, a non-profit organization that provides interview suits to low-income women seeking employment. As you can see, supporting Dress for Success really makes sense for the work I do.

◪ Offer your expert skills if you don't have the funds or the desire to write a big check. For instance, if you are a lawyer or an accountant, offer your professional services pro bono to a nonprofit.

◪ If you are just starting out, tie into a cause marketing initiative that already exists. Start with your local and national networks and get involved with charities that your colleagues and clients are supporting.

◪ Consider donating your products or gift certificates for your services to a charity auction as a way to get involved.

◪ As with any business relationship, do your homework and interview potential charity partners before committing to work with them. Make sure it is an all-around good fit.

◪ Include your charitable work on your Website and in your professional bio.

◪ Seek out PR opportunities to promote the charity and your efforts in supporting it.

◪ Consider applying for awards for civic-minded businesspeople.

◪ If your charity work involves events, ask if you can use the event mailing list to follow up with attendees who may be prospects for your business.

◪ Involve your staff in your charitable efforts and make it fun. You will achieve better results, and you will be enriching the lives of the people who work with you. The work will be more meaningful for everyone.

For more information about Mary Lou's fashionable giving, visit *www.dressingwell.com*.

Another creative cause marketer is Chris Vasiliadis, president of Signature Faces, Inc. Chris, a makeup artist, shares a press release she sent after participating in an event in which she applied makeup to women who had experienced domestic violence. Here is the press release (which was picked up by Chris's local paper, the *Burlington Union*) that tells the story.

For: Signature Faces, Inc., 114 Wilmington Road, Burlington, MA 01803

Contact: Chris Vasiliadis, chrisv@signaturefaces.com or 781-750-8350

FOR IMMEDIATE RELEASE

MOTHER'S DAY EVENT BUILDS CONFIDENCE OF DOMESTIC VIOLENCE SURVIVORS

May 10, 2004, Lowell, MA—"You lifted me up!" one participant exclaimed. On the day after Mother's Day, ten women, recent victims of domestic abuse, got a jump-start to renewed self-confidence. The Alumni Relations Council from the University of Massachusetts at Lowell, supplemented with a team of volunteers, enabled their new start.

It began in late 2003, with the Council's desire to run a community service event. They contacted Alternative House in Lowell as a possible beneficiary: Alternative House is a shelter offering comprehensive services to women and children who are victims of domestic violence. Talks started of running a springtime event near Mother's Day, to give these women a boost for returning to work or interviewing for a new job.

Suitability, a Lowell non-profit that assists women in re-entering the workforce, came on board by supplying professional suits for the women. Tom Kershaw, Council member and UMass Lowell graduate, phoned fellow alum and classmate Chris Vasiliadis, President of Burlington-based Signature Faces, Inc., to request her makeup artistry skills at the event. Chris jumped at the chance to participate, plus recruited additional volunteers. Makeup artist Linda Shields, hairstylist Michelle DeVoe, owner of Demiche Salon in Melrose, and her co-worker Alaina Dore joined the team, thrilled to contribute.

The event was a huge success! The women of Alternative House arrived in their new suits, warmly welcomed by the Council members and beauty professionals. Each participant had their choice of hairstyling, makeup or both, and all enjoyed a light dinner of sandwiches, salad, cookies and refreshments. Some women were so caught up in the excitement, that they took impromptu pictures with their makeup artist and/or hairstylist. One literally gasped with glee after seeing her new hairstyle and makeup in the mirror. All women left with not only a new look and gift of makeup supplies, but with genuine smiles and an improved outlook on themselves.

###

From Crisis, to Opportunity, to Sale, to Crisis, to Opportunity, to Sale...

As I finish writing this book I again look to the Chinese symbol for "crisis" hanging above my desk and think about all of the ups and downs we face as business owners. There are good days and bad days—and very good days and very bad days—in the sales process, but whenever I face a potential crisis I always remember that what I consider to be a crisis today could result in an enormous win tomorrow—as long as I maintain my composure and look for the opportunity and accept the danger.

I wish you all the best in your business and personal endeavors, and hope that your every pitch is perfect.

Afterword

If you've read the beginning of this book, and Bruce Nelson's foreword, you know that, in 2002, I had the good fortune and good sense of attending Office Depot's Success Strategies Conference where I bid on and won lunch with Bruce Nelson, CEO of Office Depot. My $1,050 bid went to Count-Me-In—an online micro-lending institution for women business owners, founded by Nell Merlino. Today, Office Depot remains my biggest client and Bruce Nelson one of my greatest advocates.

As this book hits the shelves of bookstores, I've had the pleasure of kicking off an initiative that has been near and dear to my heart since the time I met with Bruce Nelson: In Good Company. In Good Company is an initiative to help connect small business owners with CEOs they'd like to meet for the purposes of doing business. Through an online bidding process, entrepreneurs will have a chance to bid on lunches with CEOs and high-level executives. All proceeds will go to Count-Me-In.

Entrepreneur magazine has signed on as the media sponsor of In Good Company, providing assistance through advertising and editorial support. *Entrepreneur* hosted a luncheon in New York to launch In Good Company in June 2004. Maternity dress designer Liz Lange, who spoke at the luncheon, was so impressed with the idea of In Good Company that she offered to help by graciously donating a lunch to the cause. This initiative will be kicked-off officially in the magazine in 2005. It is my sincere hope that many of you will go to *www.ingoodcompany.com*, to see who you might make a connection with during lunch. As well as helping your own business, the proceeds raised will benefit women business owners who are unable to get funding from traditional financial sources.

Perfecting Your Pitch Top-10 Lists

As a business owner myself, I know how little time we have to read long tomes on how to run our businesses. Sometimes we just need quick reminders to solve a specific problem or reenergize our marketing and sales efforts. To that end, I have collected my best tips into top-10 lists that you can refer to when you need a boost.

1. "Before the Pitch" Top-10 Lists
Chapter 1:
Top 10 Tips for Researching Prospects

1. **Target your pitch:** Identify your top prospects by knowing the characteristics of your ideal client. Assess your relationships with past clients. Pinpoint your strengths, weaknesses, and areas of expertise. Consider your time frame and ideal location. Last, determine why your dream client should want to work with you.

2. **Know your prospects inside out:** Do your homework, so you can enter a pitch meeting fully prepared. "Google" your prospect, as well as everyone else who will be at the meeting. Thanks to the Internet, we can find out the personal and professional history of virtually anyone.

3. **Build a comprehensive database:** Keep a detailed database to manage all current and potential prospects. You'll want to utilize a contact management program, such as Best Software ACT!, where you can add notes to each contact, date all interactions, and enter personal and contact information. Keep a hard copy of this data, too. Make a file for each prospect.

4. **To buy or not to buy:** Lists generated through your own painstaking labor are best—created through networking, past clients, referrals, research, and so on. However, if you are targeting a very specific market, you may want to join a related association and purchase a list of its members. For this type of list to work, you have to be committed to making contact at least six times.

5. **Find common ground:** Use the Internet and pick up the phone to find out as much as possible about prospects. You may want to hire someone to do this research. Find out what you have in common. You might discover that he/she went to the same college as your spouse, or that you both support the same charity. Similarities help build relationships, and relationships build business.

6. **Be a secret shopper:** Perform "real world" research by shopping at your prospect's stores, using their software, or eating their food. Take notes on your experiences and enter findings into your database. Does the company have good customer service? Could they benefit from a different location?

7. **Become an avid reader:** Subscribe to essential publications, including trade magazines, a major national newspaper, a community newspaper, business magazines, your *prospect's* online newsletter and press releases, and your *competitors'* online newsletters and press releases. Scan these publications on a regular basis, to see if your prospect was quoted or featured in any of them and to keep up-to-date on general news and to know what they are reading.

8. **Become meaningfully engaged in professional organizations:** In prospecting, it is crucial to make a human connection and build face-to-face relationships. Become visible in your prospect's world by joining associations that they are involved in and being where they (and "their people") are bound to be. Become actively involved

in at least two or three organizations—those in your prospects' industries, as well as those in your own industry for peer support and best practices.

9. **Becoming meaningfully involved:** Begin by attending all of the events. Connect with association leadership by volunteering, offering your assistance in planning events, writing or editing the newsletter, and offering to speak or contribute in other ways. Try to obtain a member list, where you can find potential mentors and new prospects.

10. **Opportunities for women and minority business owners:** Join an association that will secure your business status and expose you to otherwise out-of-reach opportunities. Women can join the Women's Business Enterprise National Council (WBENC) to get certified as a woman-owned business. Minorities can join the National Minority Supplier Development Council (NMSDB), and small businesses have access to the Small Business Administration (SBA).

Chapter 2:
Top 10 Tips to Project a Professional and Memorable Visual Image

1. **Importance of a visual identity:** An appealing, memorable, and consistent visual image is imperative. Invest in a graphic designer who can create a stand-out visual identity for your business.

2. **Splurge on your logo:** Your logo will appear on all printed and electronic materials, as well as throughout your Website. It can help you to rise above the competition and be remembered. LogoWorks (*www.logoworks.com*) will create a professionally designed logo, developed with a designer's eye, for as little as $300.

3. **Business card essentials:** If you can only afford one marketing item, make it a business card, and carry it everywhere with you. Again, have it professionally designed and printed. This is what you leave behind after you meet someone. Include contact information, plus your unique selling proposition. Someone should be able to look at your card and have a clear idea of what you do in 15 seconds or less.

4. **New era of business cards:** CD-ROM business cards are becoming an increasingly popular networking tool, in addition to a paper version. Prospects can link directly to your Website, print out contact information, your bio, and so on, when they pop in the disk.

5. **Promotional kit—no more brochure:** Brochures, the most common type of promotional material, are out of date almost as soon as they're printed, but a promotional kit can easily be updated and customized for each prospect. Use a folder in your company color, with your logo printed or affixed to the front. Use high-quality paper for printed materials in the folder.

6. **What to include:** The items in your promotional kit include your biography, a history of the company, a press release, a list of services offered, client testimonials, references, a professional photograph, reprints of articles you've written and been featured in, your company newsletter, and a question-and-answer interview.

7. **What's a biography—a history of my company?** A bio is a resume written in the third person, in paragraph form, that allows no modesty. Your company history should describe what makes your company unique and should include any personal stories about how you started the business. Set out to spark the reader's interest.

8. **Testimonials explained:** Testimonials are the tools that build your reputation. If a client compliments you, ask if he or she would mind if you used the comment in your marketing materials. You can speed up the process by writing the testimonial yourself and getting your client's approval.

9. **Website, aka online promotional kit:** Your Website proves your credibility and professional existence. It should explain who you are, what you do, and what others have said about you. Include contact info at that bottom of each page. Write copy that sells (or hire someone to do this). Last, consider using autoresponders, or adding an e-commerce section to your Website.

10. **Carry your camera:** Keep a camera with you at all times to document meetings with key players in your industry and media moguls. Take photos of all speaking engagements and presentations, plus anything else that visually depicts who you are and what your company does.

Chapter 3:
Top 10 Tips to Guarantee You Get the Meeting

1. **Set your sights high:** Once you determine your dream company, contact the highest-level executive, usually the CEO. Even if he or she is not the decision-maker, they can connect you with the appropriate person and ensure that your call will be returned.

2. **Send something first:** Before making the first call, it's a good idea to send your promotional kit and a cover letter to your prospect. The initial contact by mail is unobtrusive and professional, and it gives you a reason for a follow-up phone call.

3. **Promotional kit cover letter:** Your initial letter should explain how you found this person's name and contact information (name drop!), an explanation of your business, and a short description of how you propose to help his or her business. Include compelling information to entice the recipient to read more. Conclude by saying that you will be in touch shortly. Don't forget to use what you've got! If you are a photographer, include a beautiful image on the envelope. If you design promotional gifts, send your pitch in a basket.

4. **Pre-call prep:** Wait three to five days for your package to arrive before making the call. In the meantime, decide how you will keep track of your phone calls, ideally in a contact management system, such as Best Software ACT!. Here, you will include the date and time of your call, the phone number you dialed, who you reached, the elements of your conversation, and a recommended time to call back.

5. **Determine an appropriate meeting format:** Decide what kind of a meeting you want. In some cases, you will need to have a "getting to know you" meeting, before making your pitch. In others, it is acceptable to say that you'd like to set up a meeting to explain a new product or offering. Ask yourself: "How can I offer value to my prospect in this first meeting?" and "How can I use this meeting to build a relationship?"

6. **Get in the right frame of mind:** Call when you are feeling positive. If you are stressed or anxious, your prospect will hear it in your voice. Be in business mode when you call, by sitting at your desk, calling from a landline, and clearing away all background noise. Write a mini-script, noting a few key points, to help ease your nerves.

7. **Be prepared for the ask:** Plan for a positive response. If your prospect agrees to a meeting, you need to have a plan in mind. Small business owners might appreciate an offer to take them to lunch. For a *Fortune* 500 CEO, you will want to suggest an end time. Set up a meeting for, say, 10–10:45 a.m.

8. **Find a referral:** "Warm call" your prospect. The best way to do this is to mention some sort of connection. Tell the person on the other line that his or her friend or acquaintance suggested you get in touch. If you have developed relationships through networking and being involved in the appropriate organizations, finding a referral shouldn't be difficult.

9. **Once you're on the line:** Never ask for "the head of marketing" or "the person who makes your outsourcing decisions." Confirm the correct pronunciation of your prospect's name. Find out exactly where his or her office is located, the best restaurants in the area, what type of meetings your prospect prefers, and if he or she supports a particular charity. These tidbits of information will come in handy later.

10. **CEOs don't answer their phones:** When you finally gather up the courage to make the call, it is almost a guarantee that the CEO won't answer his or her phone. You will most likely be in contact with the CEO's assistant, with whom you should become as friendly as possible. You want him or her to be your new best friend. Another tactic is to call before or after normal business hours, when the assistant is not in the office and you have a better chance of getting through directly.

Chapter 4:
Top 10 Tips for Preparing for the Pitch Meeting

1. **Send a thank-you:** After you've celebrated and taken a moment to enjoy your achievement in securing a meeting, it's time to say thank you. Send a personal, handwritten note to the person who arranged the meeting. Keep it short and sweet.

2. **Review your current marketing materials:** Review the materials you initially sent out. Has anything changed? Does client information need to be updated? If so, make necessary changes and bring your new materials to the pitch meeting.

3. **Call everyone you know:** Tap into your mastermind groups, networks, associations, and anyone else who might be able to offer information on the person or company you are pitching. Ask if they know anything about the company and if they would keep an eye out for articles about them. Also ask their advice on anything you may be overlooking or need to work on.

4. **Play 20 questions:** Plan to ask a lot of questions in the meeting. The best questions explore *new* developments about your prospect, allow prospects to talk about their companies or themselves, and provide insights into their biggest concerns.

5. **Design a clear and concise visual presentation:** Always bring a presentation to the meeting. Microsoft PowerPoint works particularly well to illustrate points. Bring a hard copy and CD-ROM version. Presentations should be clear, succinct, professional, and customized. Offer background information; share your personal story; use statistics, diagrams, and visuals; and include references and relevant press clippings.

6. **Rehearse:** Practice your presentation in front of trusted advisors, friends, and family. It is a good idea to videotape and analyze the presentation content, style, and length, as well as your appearance.

7. **Plan your appearance:** A professional appearance matters. Invest in professional items, such as a leather portfolio and classic pen. Dress conservatively, have a pulled-together hairstyle, don't wear outlandish accessories, and allow time for any regular grooming activities, such as a manicure.

8. **Check your credit card balance:** If you are taking your prospect out to lunch, surely you will be footing the bill. You should expect to pay for travel expenses to and from your prospect's place of business, too, so plan ahead to avoid a potentially embarrassing situation.

9. **Confirm your appointment:** Call a few days ahead of time to confirm the time and location of the meeting. This will most likely be done through your prospect's assistant. Avoid contacting your prospect after this phone call—you don't want to seem like a pest.

10. **Plan to arrive early:** This is the day you've been waiting for, so there is no excuse for being late. Expect traffic and other delays. You can always wait in your car for a few minutes before the meeting, if you arrive early.

II. During the Pitch Top 10 Lists
Chapter 5:
Top 10 Tips for First-Rate Presentations

1. **Visual appeal:** To make your PowerPoint presentation more appealing to the audience, use mainly visual images, as opposed to text. Crisp photos are generally a better choice than clipart. Photos are more professional and modern looking.

2. **Text basics:** Use at least a 20-point font, so text is legible by the audience. Play up text by using different colors and sizes to accentuate certain words, but don't have too much going on at once. White space is necessary, and you should use it to your advantage to make points. Don't include too many images and words or your audience will get lost.

3. **Font facts:** Use a generic font that is installed on all computers, such as Arial, Times, or Verdana. Otherwise, when you open your presentation at a speaking event, words might appear jumbled and distorted. If you really want to use a different font, this issue usually can be avoided when you save your presentation. Select "save options" or "general options" and then choose "embed true type fonts." I recommend using no more than two font types in a presentation, to keep it consistent.

4. **Consistent background or template that reflects your identity:** If you are not very PowerPoint savvy, invest in a designer to create a template that can be used in all of your PowerPoint presentations. The template should include your company colors, logo, and contact information. If you are creating your own background, use the program's slide master view (access the "view" menu, select "master," and then select "slide master"). Choose background from the format menu and select a color. Insert your logo on top or bottom and include contact information at the bottom of the slide.

5. **Logical order:** Compile your presentation in an order that will make sense to your audience. You are an expert on the topic, but put yourself in the shoes of someone learning the information for the first time. Go through your presentation ahead of time and rehearse out loud.

6. **Make your point:** Each slide should represent a key point that you want to make. Include basic information on the slides that will reinforce your message. Elaborate on the points when speaking. Images should stimulate a visual connection to the points being addressed.

7. **Illustrate your point with stories:** Include a personal connection or an example, whenever possible. This is guaranteed to make your presentation more engaging and will show your human side, which people appreciate.

8. **Bring people back to your Website for additional information on the subject:** Write a white paper or article that is tied into your presentation and that reinforces the information you spoke about. Make it available on your Website for attendees to download after your seminar and send to the media. Make audience members aware of additional resources and items of interest that are available at your Website for a compelling reason for them to revisit you.

9. **Create handouts that compliment your presentation:** A handout is easy to make. Start with a cover page that includes the title of your presentation, your name and contact information, and the logo of the organization or group you are presenting to. You may want to include your bio or a related article, as well. After that, print out

handouts of your PowerPoint presentation, with three to nine slides per page. Do this by selecting "print." Next, from the "print what" menu, select "handouts" and choose the number you want to print per page. Black and white is acceptable. Never give your handout to an attendee until the *end* of your presentation. The audience, too often, will focus on the handout, not on what you're trying to impart to them.

10. **Save your presentation and have a backup plan:** When your PowerPoint presentation is completed, save it as a PowerPoint Show and burn it to a CD, so it is self-starting. You can save it as a PowerPoint Show by accessing the "file" menu, selecting "save as," and then selecting "PowerPoint Show (*.pps)" from the "save as type" menu. Always be prepared for the worst, and have a backup plan. Your presentation will most likely be too large to e-mail, so you should upload it to a file-sharing server from which you can download it in an emergency.

Chapter 6:
Top 10 Tips for Writing a Winning Proposal

1. **Show them that you heard them:** Hopefully you really listened to what your prospect had to say during your meeting. Now is your chance to prove that you heard them. Find out how your prospect wants you to format your proposal, then be sure to include details on the program you are pitching, benefits of hiring you, the expected cost, a timeline, stories of satisfied customers, your bio, relevant media you've been featured in, and references.

2. **The format:** The length of your proposal should be in accordance with what your prospect requested. In any case, if they did not make a specific request, it should be as succinct as possible. Make it readable with clear headlines; bullet points; illustrations; and bold, capital, or underlined emphasis of key points.

3. **Benchmarks:** Know your prospect's main issues. If your prospect cares most about low fees, quick turnaround, or superior quality, reflect those success factors in your proposal.

4. **Nonstarters:** Know what to exclude. If you learned that your prospect is interested only in a specific service that you provide, do not detail everything you have to offer, no matter how beneficial you think it would be. If you do a superior job, there may be an interest in the future.

5. **Language:** Refer to specific comments that were made at the meeting and use some of the terms and acronyms that attendees used—it shows that you were listening. It is also acceptable to use industry jargon.

6. **News:** Demonstrate that you are keeping up on all news about your prospect's industry or company by referencing any new developments, product launches, or news stories about the company in your proposal.

7. **Additional information:** Now is another good time to speak with friends and colleagues about their experiences with the company you are pitching. Compare notes on what happened during your first meeting.

8. **Numbers:** Take some time to consider how you will incorporate information on price, deliverables, and timing. If possible, avoid talking price in your first follow-up proposal. This is a discussion that you should have over the phone to ensure that you are on the same page.

9. **Letter of agreement:** If you are ready to close the deal, include a letter of agreement as an attachment at the end of your written proposal. Consult with your lawyer to create this.

10. **The look and feel:** As always, be consistent. The look and tone should be similar to previous written materials and should be easy to recognize. Personalize the pitch with the company's logo, your contact's name, and other indicators. Proofread and show your proposal to trusted advisors for edits.

Chapter 7:
Top 10 Tips for Being Persistent

1. **Establish your desired reach and frequency of contact:** This is your "persistence plan," and it will depend on several factors. First, depending on the size of the organization you are pitching, your proposal may need to be approved by several layers of people, but no

matter what, you should always correspond with your main contact. It may also depend on your prospect's personal style, whether they are meeting with your competition, the economy, and the calendar. If you pitched just before the December holidays, you may have to wait awhile for a response.

2. **Smart, simple, tried and true tactics:** Immediately following your meeting, send a one-page recap of action times and delivery dates. Offer to help your prospect in some way, free of charge, or send a marketing tip or a suggestion that you did not mention in the meeting.

3. **Send articles of interest:** Check newspapers, magazines, industry publications, and online newsletters daily for information that may be of interest to your prospect. Forward it with a brief note, but don't mention your proposal.

4. **Inform your prospect of accomplishments and recognize theirs:** Toot your own horn and share updates on new clients, new products, positive press, and new employee hires. On the same note, recognize any mention of your prospect's company in the news or company developments with a note of congratulations.

5. **Invite your prospect to events:** Invite your prospect to be your guest at an event in a nonmeeting setting. Check your local newspaper or chamber of commerce listings for events. Even if he or she declines, you have proven yourself to be connected, generous, and dedicated to deepening your relationship.

6. **Show up where your prospect might be:** Attend industry events, association meetings, chamber of commerce functions, or any event where you think your prospect or his or her colleagues may be.

7. **Connect through mutual contacts:** Call a mutual acquaintance to say hello and update them on your potential deal. As a result, they might casually mention you the next time they run into your prospect.

8. **Show that you have a good memory:** Remember specific details from your meeting and facts about your prospect. If his or her birthday falls during the waiting period, don't hesitate to send a card.

9. **Be pleasantly persistent without being obnoxious:** If you still haven't gotten a response after the agreed-upon time frame, don't panic or jump to conclusions. You can anonymously check up on your prospect by phoning the receptionist or an assistant. Attempt to make one contact each by phone, cell phone, and e-mail. Wait one week and follow up again.

10. **Creative follow-up tactics:** You are sure to get your prospect's attention by doing something similar to what Stephanie Cohen and Hayley Byer of Verge Promotional Marketing do: They move their deals closer to closing by sending a cute flower pot containing soil and seeds. The attached note reads, "We want to grow your business."

III. After the Pitch Top 10 Lists
Chapter 8:
Top 10 Tips for Effective Surveying

1. **Surveying is marketing:** Surveying clients should be part of your marketing plan and should be done at least annually, but ideally, every six months. It is a way to receive valuable feedback on what adjustments you should make to your business, as well as a chance to gain some new testimonials.

2. **State your goal:** There are a variety of reasons why you might want to survey your clients. Among the most common are to identify pricing perceptions, determine clients' feelings about your customer service, and to find out their views about your product or service.

3. **Quantitative vs. qualitative:** This decision should be based on your goal and the volume of customers that you have. Qualitative surveys are open-ended and result in much deeper information. Quantitative surveys seek out numerical, quantifiable data and are best suited for surveying large volumes.

4. **Choose your method:** You may choose to use an unbiased third party human surveyor to elicit honest and in-depth information. Online surveys are another option that are cheap and easy to create. They can be limited in scope, but offer both quantitative and qualitative

questions. Zoomerang.com is my choice for online surveying. A third option is to send a survey by mail, but this can be costly and time-consuming, and it requires aggressive follow-up.

5. **Create the questions:** Be very direct and specific. Ask questions that can only be interpreted one way. Sample questions include:

   ◪ What specific value have you received?

   ◪ What are the strengths of this organization and its service or product?

   ◪ Can you quantify the value of working with us?

   ◪ Would you be willing to provide a testimonial?

6. **Introduce the survey:** Contact the people you plan to survey. Let them know what you are doing, that their feedback is important, and what they will be asked. It is a nice personal touch. You don't want clients to be surprised by a phone call from a third-party surveyor or when they receive something in the mail.

7. **Follow up and encourage response:** If you've sent your survey by mail or e-mail, follow up with another e-mail saying, "There's one more week until we begin to evaluate the responses. We'd appreciate your feedback. Please don't forget about it!" People tend to put off surveys.

8. **Express your gratitude in writing:** Follow up with a thank-you to clients who take the time to participate in your survey. By letting them know you appreciate your help, you are building customer loyalty.

9. **Collect and organize your data:** Once you receive feedback, it is time to organize it, analyze the results, determine what it means to your business, and create an action list of changes you are going to make.

10. **Communicate your action plan:** Show clients that you took their comments to heart and are serious about your business. Send out a letter saying, "We did this survey. We received this kind of feedback. Thank you to everyone who participated, and here's what were going to do as a result of this feedback."

Chapter 9:
Top 10 Tips for a Successful Endorsement Campaign

1. **Endorsements vs. testimonials:** Both are written from your client's perspective. The difference is that an endorsement goes directly from your client to your prospects, on their letterhead, saying how wonderful your product or service is.

2. **Tier 1—Identify your best client:** The first step of an endorsement campaign is to find your best client, who would be willing to send a letter on your behalf. Choose a longtime client who has clearly indicated his or her satisfaction with you. Assure your client that you will not "outgrow" his or her business and explain that it is an opportunity to improve your client's reputation as well. Show your gratitude often.

3. **Write it on your client's behalf:** This relieves the burden from your client and offers you the opportunity to include exactly what you want. Be sure to incorporate several bullet points, facts, and statistics. Offer a recommendation that your prospects can't refuse. Then, send it to your client to review and sign off on. The letter should be no more than two to three pages long and I suggest offering a freebie with it, such as a book you have authored or a sample of your product.

4. **Create a killer prospect list:** By now, you should already have a list of dream clients. Now that you have won at least one of them, it is time to update the list. Your client may even recommend people to add to the list.

5. **Give clients the final review:** Allow your client to review and edit the letter, as well as to make changes to your prospect list as he or she sees fit—it's only fair.

6. **Offer to return the favor:** Graciously assure your client that you would be happy to return the favor in the future. They may not ask you to write an endorsement letter, but they might call you up in need of a sponsor for the marathon they are running. It is well worth it.

7. **The mailing:** Collect your client's company letterhead so you can do the mailing yourself. If they are from out of state, I highly suggest taking a trip to their location, so the postmark comes from their town. Another option is to hire a virtual assistant to do the mailing for you. Handwrite your prospects' names on the envelopes and send them out by standard first-class mail.

8. **Tier 2—Follow-up letter from you:** The next tier after sending out your client's endorsement letter is to send a follow-up letter from you, within two to three weeks. At the beginning of the letter, remind them of your client's generosity in sending a letter out on your behalf. Reiterate the points that were made in the initial letter and remind prospects of what you did for that client. Include two to three more testimonials, a coupon or giveaway, and a fax-back form.

9. **Tier 3—Final follow-up:** Two to three weeks later, send a final letter to prospects who have not responded yet. Let them know, once again, how grateful you are to your client, that you understand they must be busy, and outline what you can do for them. Include a copy of your client's original letter, a fax-back form, and another giveaway item or valuable resource.

10. **Final follow-up calls:** Last, make personal phone calls to prospects who you have not heard from. You may learn of a specific committee dedicated to handling your type of inquiry or an alternate contact and will be able to grow your database.

Chapter 10:
Top 10 Ways to Use Creativity in Your Marketing Efforts

1. **Hire a designer:** You need to find someone to create a wonderful identity for your business. Ask people whose logos you admire who they use for their identity and get samples of their work.

2. **Offer up a creative tag line:** Develop a slogan for your business that is result-focused. Think of Nike's "Just Do It."

3. **Keep an open mind:** Be aware of and open to new opportunities and be prepared to pounce on them when they show up.

4. **Do the unexpected:** Don't send a holiday card out in December—everyone else does. Think of another holiday or event you can acknowledge, to separate you from the pack.

5. **Read a thought-inspiring book:** Buy a book such as *ThinkerToys* or—my own book—*Off the Wall Marketing Ideas,* to get your juices going.

6. **Creative promotional items:** Visit a toy shop to get ideas for promotional items you might give away to clients, or keep an eye out at trade shows or other events.

7. **Broaden perception:** Attend a marketing seminar and try to relate the situations or examples to your business.

8. **Effective copy:** Work with a copywriter who can make your words sing, be easily repeatable, and succinct.

9. **Appearance:** Think about your appearance and whether it reflects your business accurately. A few years ago, at the Academy Awards, a woman who won for best costume design came onto the stage wearing an American Express Gold Card dress. I never forgot that, and it spoke volumes about her profession and creative talent.

10. **Planning:** Write a simple-to-follow plan filled with simply creative ideas and follow it through.

Index

A

action plan, communicating your, 175-176

agenda,
    preparing an, 121-124
    sample, 122

Allen, Lauren, 45-47

Andre, Mary Lou, 219-222

announcing your new client
    relationship, 163-164
    to your staff and business
        partners, 164-165

appearance, planning your
    presentation, 115-116

appointment, confirming your,
    116-117

arrival time, for your presentation, 117

articles, reprints of, as part of
    promotional kit, 64

assistants, working with prospects',
    101-103

Attiliis, Andy, 105

audience, finding your, 214

autoresponders, 206

B

Best Software ACT!, 28

biography, your, 54

Blakely, Sara, 98

Block, Kerstin and Spencer, 215

brochures, 53-54

Buffalo Exchange, 215-216

building buzz, 145, 179

business cards, importance of
    having, 51-53

Business Networking International
    (BMI), 81

buzz, building, 145,179

C

calendars as direct mail, 212

calls, keeping track of, 93

camera, having with you at all times, 72-73

Cantando, Mary, 97-98

CD-ROM
business cards, 53
version of your presentation, 112

challenge to your business, 128-129

challenges, responding to, 128-133

characteristics of clients, identifying, 25

client testimonials, 64

clients, questions about former, 130-131

Cloth Envelope Company, The, 91-92, 213

company history, as part of promotional kit, 54

concept, having a creating direct mail, 208-209

confidence, importance of, 117

consistency, in marketing, 197-198

contacting your prospect, alternate routes to, 104-105

contacts, building and organizing, 218-219

contract, 140-143
sample, 141-143

Count-Me-In, 225

credit card balance, checking your, 116

customers, keeping for life, 176-178

D

Darling, Diane, 117

data, collecting and organizing survey, 175

database lists, purchasing, 29-30

database,
building a strong, 200
developing a comprehensive, 28-31

deadlines, importance of meeting, 166

delivery of your proposal, 143-144

direct mail, 208-214
ease in replying to, 214
formats for, 210-211
invitations as, 212
postcards as, 210-212
writing catching copy for, 209

Do-It-Yourself Direct-Mail Handbook, The, 209

E

educating your new client, 166

Effective Networking, Inc., 117

elevator pitch, 45-49

endorsement campaign
tier one, 180-188
tier three, 191-195
tier two, 188-191

endorsement campaign,
creating an, 179-195
final follow-up as part of, 188-191
three-tiered, 180-194
top 10 tips for a successful, 241-242

endorsement letter,
sample, 184-187
preparing, 180-184

endorsements vs. testimonials, 180

endorser, choosing your, 180

Entrepreneur, 225

entrepreneurship as career alternative, 11

envelopes, using intriguing, 213

equipment, testing out prior to your presentation, 125

Erdman, Ken, 209
expert, becoming a published, 216-217
expertise, when yours is questioned, 130
e-mail and legal issues, 200
e-zines, 199-202
    sample, 201, 202-205

F

Fathelbab, Mohammed, 81
feedback, requesting, 168-170
15SecondPitch, 45-47
final follow-up, as part of
    endorsement campaign, 188-191
first five minutes, importance of the,
    125-126
follow-up,
    determining method of, 149-151
    final, as part of endorsement
        campaign, 191-195
    mistakes to avoid in your, 152
follow-up
    action plan, developing a, 149
    letter, as part of endorsement
        campaign, 188-189
    sample, 189-191
    strategies, 151
    tactics, creative, 158-159
formats for direct mail, 210-211
Forum Resources Network, 81
Fredrickson, Fabienne, 123, 136
free reports, 206
Fusion Sales Partners, 111

G

Gillen, Mary, 105
Gimme the Skinny, 93

gimmicks, 215-216
giving back, 219
goal of the survey, stating your, 170-171
Groop, Peter, 111

H

Hill, Napoleon, 80
holidays, celebrating nontraditional,
    214-215

I

ideal client, identifying your, 25-26
In Good Company, 225-226
industry leaders, identifying, 73-77
invitations as direct mail, 212

K

Kabachnick, Terri, 96-97

L

LaPlante Dube, Susan, 170-172
LeBlanc, Mark, 26
legal issues and e-mail, 200
letters, direct mail, 210
lifelong marketing, 197-224
logo, importance of having a, 49-51
LogoWorks, 49

M

mailed surveys, 173
marketing creatively, top 10 tips for,
    242-243
marketing materials, reviewing
    your, 110
marketing, lifelong, 197-224

mastermind group,
    creating a, 80-83
        suggestions for, 82-83
    using for meeting prep, 110
meeting format, deciding on a, 96-98
meeting,
    deterioration of a, 132-133
    getting the, 85-100
    preparing for your, 109-117
    top 10 tips to getting the, 231-232
    top 10 tips to preparing the pitch
        for, 233-234
Melanson, Maggie, 93
Merlino, Nell, 26, 74-75, 225
Microsoft Outlook, 28
mistakes to avoid in your follow-up, 152
Mixed Media Publicity & Promotion,
    156
multicultural markets, translating
    Website for, 207

N

Nelson, Bruce, 14, 16, 19, 85, 112,
    219, 225
networking with prospects, 4-44
newsletter, company, 64
next steps, discussing with your
    prospect, 133-134
Nine Lives, 97

O

Off the Wall Marketing Ideas, 182
offers, enticing, 213
Office Depot Web Café, 166-168
Office Depot, 11, 13-16, 19, 74, 112,
    219, 225
online contests, 207

online presence, perfecting your,
    199-205
online surveys, 173
overdelivery, 161-178

P

"persistence plan," 149
persistence, gentle, 149-159
persistent,
    remaining pleasantly, 154-157
    top 10 tips for being, 237-239
photograph, as part of promotional
    kit, 64
pitch, elevator, 45-49
pitching over a meal, 126-127
Pollak, Jane, 14, 19
postcards as direct mail, 210-212
pre-call prep, 93-95
Precision Marketing Group, 170
pre-deal bonuses, 144-145
preparation, importance of, 99-100
presentation
    content, 113-115
    do's and don'ts, 112-113
presentation,
    rehearsing your, 115
    top 10 tips for first-rate, 234-236
    visual, designing a, 112-115
press releases, 54
    sample, 55-59, 17-19, 77-79
price, when a client asks prematurely
    about, 129-130
professional organizations for
    women and minorities, 36-38
professional organizations,
    becoming involved in, 35-36
    joining, 34-41

promises, fulfilling, 161
promotional kit, 53-68
    cover letter samples for, 89-91
    sending to prospects, 88-93
proposal
    content, 138-140
    delivery, 143-144
    format,
        elements of the, 136-143
        learning your prospect's
            preferred, 135-136
proposal,
    submitting an outstanding, 135-145
    the look and feel of the, 140
    top 10 tips for writing winning,
        236-237
prospect list, creating a, 182
prospects,
    interviewing, 97
    researching, 28-41
public speaking as marketing tool, 217
publications, subscribing to, 33
published, becoming, 216-217

Q

qualitative vs. quantitative surveys,
    171-172
question-and-answer interview, 65
    sample, 65-68
questions,
    asking, 111-112, 127-128
        about former clients, 130-101
    survey, creating your, 173-174

R

Raphel, Murray, 209
Ready to Wear, 219

references, list of, 64
referrals, getting, 86-88
rehearsing your presentation, 115
relationship,
    building, 43-83
    developing a, with your new
        client, 161-162
repetition, in marketing, 197-198
replying to direct mail, ease in, 214
reprints of articles for promotional
    kits, 64
reporting methods, develop regular,
    166-168
reputation,
    building your, 43-83
    elements of a good, 44-73
research,
    formal client, 169
    soliciting informal client, 169-170
researching prospects,
    guide to, 28-41
    top 10 tips to, 227-229
resource, remaining a, for your
    prospect, 152-154
"Rule of AIDA," 209
Rules of 4 and 6, 198-199

S

Safar Coiffure, 213
Safar, Serge, 213
Sawyer, Carolyn, 149
Scharmen, Rose, 91
services, list of, 59
    sample, 59-63
Shea, Ginny, 156
Signature Faces, Inc., 222-224
Slutsky, Jeff, 214

small business, when a large
company questions working with
a, 131-132
Staples, 182
Streetfighter Marketing, 214
survey
data, collecting and organizing, 175
follow-up, 175
method, choosing the right,
172-173
participation, thanking for, 175
questions, creating your, 173-174
surveys,
additional benefits of, 176
as marketing tool, 170-176
introducing, 174-175
mailed, 173
online, 173
stating goals of, 170-171
third-party, 172-173
top 10 tips for effective, 239-240

T

teaching as marketing tool, 217-218
team, understanding your
prospects', 106-107
telephone logs, sample, 94-95
tell-a-friend, 206-207
testimonials, 64
vs. endorsements, 180
thank-you notes, 110
Think and Grow Rich, 80
third-party surveys, 172-173
Throckmorton, Joan, 209
Tom Sawyer Company, 149
top-10 tips lists, 227-243

U

unique selling proposition (USP),
25-27

V

value, understanding your client's
definition of, 169
Vasiliadis, Chris, 222
VCR, as foundation of marketing,
197-198, 206-207
visibility, in marketing, 197-198
visible, remaining, 214
visual image, top 10 tips to
projecting a professional and
memorable, 229-230
voice mail, prospects', 103-104

W

Web marketing strategies,
additional, 206
Website,
importance of having a, 68-72
translating for multicultural
markets, 207
Winfrey, Oprah, 93
*Winning Direct Response
Advertising*, 209

Y

Young Entrepreneurs
Organization, 81

About the Author

NANCY MICHAELS is the president of Impression Impact, a marketing consulting firm in Concord, Massachusetts. She works with *Fortune* 1000 companies, targeting the small business marketplace, and is the creator of a multimedia platform—Grow Your Business (*www.growyourbusinesstour.com*)—that provides client coaching, seminars, webcasts, and relevant content and resources to small business owners.

Nancy is the author of two books on marketing for small businesses: *Perfecting Your Pitch* (Career Press, 2005) and *Off the Wall Marketing Ideas*, (Adams Media, 2000), as well as three self-published resource guides: *How to Be a Big Fish in Any Pond, Media Madness*, and *A to Z to Visibility*. She is the Small Business Editor at *U.S. News & World Report*, the Small Business Marketing Expert for *Entrepreneur* magazine, and has been featured in *The Wall Street Journal*, *Fortune Small Business (FSB)*, *Success Magazine*, *The New York Post*, and *Franchising Magazine*, among numerous other publications.

Impression Impact's clients include Office Depot, Xerox, Merrill Lynch, JPMorgan Chase, Cendant, Card Services International, UPS, Constant Contact, LogoWorks, and many others. In addition, Nancy's company produces Office Depot.com's Web Café Series of online seminars geared toward small business owners.

In 2002, Nancy was the first recipient to win the Tom Peters WOW! Project Personified Award that hails individuals who take on WOW! projects. She and her speaker team have conducted more than 600 seminars in three years on behalf of a national retailer, where sales increased 200 to 300 percent on the days of these events.

Previously, Nancy was a nationally syndicated newspaper small business columnist for Scripps-Howard News Service. Nancy also was the publicist for Matt Lauer (current cohost of the *Today* show).

She lives in Concord, Massachusetts, with her husband and three small children. You can reach Nancy, regarding her coaching services, speaking engagements, and consulting practice by visiting *www.impressionimpact.com.*